BLACK POWER

STRATEGIES FOR ACHIEVING AND UTILIZING POWER IN AMERICA

MICHAEL ALAN TOWNSEND

BRONX VILLAGE PUBLISHERS
P.O. BOX 1021
BRONX, NY 10466

I

Publishers Note
This publication is designed to provide accurate and authoritative information in regard to the subject matter covered. It is sold with the understanding that the publisher is not engaged in rendering psychological, financial, legal, or other professional services. If expert assistance or counseling is needed, the services of a competent professional should be sought.

Published by Bronx Village Publishers
P.O. Box 1021
Bronx NY 10466

Library of Congress Control Number: 2004103373
ISBN 0-9753205-0-5

Printed in the United States of America

Dedication

This book is dedicated to my mother, Madeline Townsend. You provided me with the physical, intellectual, and spiritual nourishment that made me the person I am today. Even though you're gone, I will never write a word I don't want you to read.

Acknowledgments

First and foremost I would like to thank my wife Margaret. When I was ready to quit she gave me the confidence to go on. You never stopped believing in me, and for that I am truly grateful.

I would also like to thank Uncle Davey and Aunt Cheryl. True role models and proof there is light at the end of the tunnel.

Table of contents

Chapter 1
Power = Freedom

Physical slavery ended in the United States in 1865, with the ratification of the 13th amendment to the Constitution. Never the less, this evil institution still affects the economic, psychological and sociological conditions of African Americans to this day. This list does not include every ailment left over from physical slavery; but virtually everything that affects African Americans as a group can be connected to one of these three. Some would even argue that because of this, slavery still exists, in all, but it's physical form. It will be shown that, although the physical chains are gone, there still exist virtual chains. One of the problems with these virtual chains is those enslaved by them, most often don't know it.

It most be pointed out that there are many people of African decent in America who don't consider themselves African American. This group mostly consists of people born in the Caribbean or on the Continent of Africa itself. Also included in this group are many people of Hispanic origin. Members of these groups often become confused and disillusioned when their children or grand children suffer the same plight as the native African Americans. It is therefore important for them to recognize that these issues affect them also.

In this book these virtual chains will be called not surprisingly, the Economic, Psychological and Sociological chains. Another set of terms that will be used in this book are; House Slave, Field Slave and Free Man. These are defined as follows.

The House Slave was most often was a slave that lived in the plantation owners house, or at least separate from the other slaves. Sometimes the House Slave would belong to a master who was not a plantation owner. These were the slaves that belonged to ship captains, slave traders etc. If the master was rich enough, these slaves often lived better than some whites. It was usually the House Slave that told master about plans to revolt or escape. The modern analogy of a House Slave is one, who has been let into society, under the condition that he does not forget his place. For example; If Secretary of State Colin Powell made a public announcement that African Americans were owed a debt for slavery and that he favored reparations, what do you think would happen? It's a pretty good chance he'd be kicked out the (White) House. A very important rule for a House Slave is, watch your mouth. Also the House Slave must imitate some of the master's customs, morals and values. More accurately they must give up language and customs that are radically different or not easily understood by the master. An example of this would be; National Security Adviser Condelisa Rice shows up at the (White) House with her hair done in Dreadlocks, wearing African style clothing. How long do you think she would be accepted in Bush's (White) House? The House Slave often though not always, tends to be better off financially and educationally than the Field Slave.

Next we have the Field Slave. This is the category that the majority of African Americans fall into. To fully understand the field slave we must remember that during the period of Physical Slavery, there were varied conditions under which the slaves lived. You had the most recognized form, the Plantation Slave; picking cotton, living in slave quarters, eating Chitterlings and singing spirituals. The Plantation Slave wasn't happy, but for the most part accepted his condition. Many tried to escape. Some would even attempt to revolt. It would be interesting to note that according to the Encyclopedia Britannica, there were over two hundred slave revolts in the United States, where ten or more slaves attempted to fight for freedom. The most famous, but yet not the biggest was Nat Turner's revolt. The modern day analogy of Field Slave is the life that African Americans are basically living, they toil and labor for master's benefit, never surpassing the master. Hence you find the Field Slaves in low income housing projects, slums and prisons. These are the new slave quarters'. Illegal street drugs, limited access to education and sub-standard medical care are some of the whips used to keep these slaves in line. Some of the modern day Field Slaves are highly educated and hold good jobs or profitable businesses. These are the hardest ones to convince that they are still enslaved. Often times it takes an overt act of racism and or violence to remind them of their place in society. The Reverend Dr. Martin Luther King is an example of a Field Slave going too far in rallying the slaves. This led to his assassination. Malcolm X (Al-Hajj Malik Shabazz) is an example of a Field Slave trying to lead a revolt against the status quo. In his case they used other slaves to lynch/assassinate him.

Finally we have the Free Man. Webster defines free as: having the legal and political rights of a citizen.

Freedom is also defined as: the quality or state of being free; the absence of necessity, coercion or constraint in choice or action.

In other words you are free to make whatever choices you want, or at the very least you have the same choices as other citizens.

Now lets take a look a deeper look at the definition of freedom; having the legal and political rights of a citizen, and freedom of choice.

The 13th, 14th and 15th amendments to the U.S. Constitution supposedly ended physical slavery, granted equality and gave former slaves the right to vote... They read as follows;

Amendment 13
(Ratified Dec. 6, 1865)
Section 1

Neither slavery, nor involuntary servitude, except as punishment for crime whereof the party shall have been duly convicted, shall exist within the United States, or any place subject to their jurisdiction.

Section 2
Congress shall have the power to enforce this article by appropriate legislation.

Amendment 14
(Ratified July 9, 1868)
Section 1
All persons born or naturalized in the United States, and subject to the jurisdiction thereof, are citizens of the United States and of the state wherein they reside. No state shall make or enforce any law which shall abridge the privileges or immunities of citizens of the United States, nor shall any state deprive any person of life, liberty, of property, without due process of law; nor deny any person within its jurisdiction the equal protection of the laws.....

Amendment 15

(Ratified Feb. 3, 1870)
Section 1
The rights of citizens to vote shall not be denied or abridged by the United States or by any state on account

of race, color or previous condition of servitude….

The problem was that after reconstruction[1]; the plantation owners, businessmen and lawmakers in the south quickly found ways around these amendments.

Slavery was replaced with Sharecropping.

Jim Crow style, "Separate but equal" laws helped them get around the 14th Amendment.

Literacy requirements in which Blacks had to pass reading test to vote, Grandfather clauses which helped illiterate whites to vote, and Poll taxes which forced Blacks to pay a voters tax on Election Day, helped them around the 15th Amendment, thus preventing the descendants of the former slaves from voting.

These institutions denied African Americans many of the civil rights enjoyed by whites, therefore, denying them freedom according to Webster's' definition.

It wasn't until the 1954 Supreme Court ruling in Brown vs. Board of Education[2], that the Federal government made any serious attempt to desegregate public schools in the Deep South.

The 24th Amendment (Ratified Jan 23, 1964) eliminated all forms of poll tax[3].

---

[1] The period after the Civil War in which the former Confederate states where eased back into United States.

[2] This was the ruling that declared that "separate but equal" was unconstitutional.

[3] A tax that one must pay before they can vote.

We can see that nearly one hundred years after the "legal" ending of Physical Slavery; new laws had to be enacted just to enforce the old laws. Many have come to the conclusion that all the new laws in the world won't completely change the condition of Africans in America. What is really needed is a change of attitudes and behaviors, both for Blacks as well as whites.

Those who would want us enslaved find more sophisticated ways to cleverly circumvent any and all laws that give us freedom/equality. In the chapters that follow, it will be shown how African Americans can become equally as clever and sophisticated in breaking these chains that hold us down.

Also be advised, that the lock that holds these chains to our people is ignorance. The only true way to break this lock is through the acquisition of knowledge. Therefore an attempt will be made to explain the workings of the three chains, i.e. the Economic, Psychological, and Sociological aspects, and how African Americans can utilize this knowledge.

There is no doubt that the Europeans have excelled in both the physical and social sciences for the last 400 years. It is not surprising that the three chains are branches of the Social Sciences. Some of the others being, Anthropology, History, Law, and Political Science. You will find that all these fields of knowledge are tied together. There is a glossary at the end of this book, which will explain these terms.

It's also important to distinguish between the two types of freedom.

The first type is the runaway slave freedom. Slave owning societies considered this type of freedom illegitimate. The slave on the run was free as long as he wasn't caught. This type of freedom was difficult to maintain. If captured the slave was often punished publicly. This was to convince the other slaves that running away wasn't worth the risk.

The second type is total freedom. The people who had this status were legally considered free. In other words they had the rights of a free member of the society.

Today African Americans have the illusion of being free, but lack the power of the truly free. In a sense, they are just modern day runaway slaves. They are protected by Civil Rights laws and Racial Quotas, which are at present time being threatened with being repealed. In other words, their status as equal citizens is in jeopardy. To gain true freedom African Americans must be willing to follow in the footsteps of those like Nat Turner. It is not being suggested that they go to arms and start killing people; instead it should be a strategic and mental fight. Freedom must be won, 400 years in America has shown us that it will not be granted without a struggle. Remember when a slave breaks for freedom, there's always a posse giving chase.

Freedom's price

We often hear about the price of freedom. This term is often used by political leaders when they want to justify the deaths of American soldiers.

We too must pay the price for our own freedom here in America. It will take a commitment of courage, discipline, and perseverance. Let's examine these three character traits.

✗**Courage.** First off we'll determine what courage is not. Courage is not the absence of fear. This is called fearlessness; it is similar to courage but not the same. To be fearless means you don't understand or recognize the danger that exists in a situation. It's like little children who find their parents hand gun. If young and naive enough they will play with this gun fearlessly. This state is born from ignorance. Remember ignorance is the lock that holds our chains in place. Courage on the other hand is the mental or moral strength to act in spite of danger, fear, or difficulty. The man who runs into a burning building to save a trapped child is courageous. He knows the potential consequences of his actions. To be courageous you must know the danger in the situation you face.

We must keep in mind that courage must be balanced with restraint. The prisons and grave yards are full of brave young African Americans. Fear can be a warning that things may not work out for you in a favorable way. You have to determine if it is a protective fear or a paralyzing one.

Preparation kills fear. This is the main reason armies train. What good is a well equipped army if it is terrified? Therefore if you plan to work towards any goal you must prepare. You must find out what it is you will be facing. If there are books on the subject try to read them. There's an old saying, "if you want to hide knowledge from a Black man, put it in a book. Let's make this saying a lie.

Discipline. Discipline can be described as the ability to stay focused. It is self-control, the ability to avoid being distracted.

In our quest to gain Freedom there are many distractions. They come in many forms. The two most devastating are drugs and Black on Black violent crime.

It is no coincidence that drugs hit the African American community in a big way, when the civil rights movement started. As Black people finally became united, drugs started to enter the community. This has since become a major distraction.

For many Blacks, their whole lives are centered on the buying or selling of drugs. These people have family members who are also affected. Remember there was no war on drugs until white America's children started shooting heroin, and smoking Crack.

We've all heard that Black on Black crime has reached epidemic proportions. What we don't hear is how it distracts us from advancing as a people. This problem will be discussed in detail later.

Perseverance. To win the fight for our freedom we must persevere. Samuel Johnson said, "Great works are preformed not by strength, but by perseverance." Perseverance is the ability to stay the course. It's mental endurance. Don't confuse perseverance with tolerance. Perseverance is the ability to endure a course of action that is of benefit to you. Tolerance is putting up with someone else's behavior, which usually benefits them. Simply put, perseverance is your choice to endure a situation, whereas tolerance is someone or something else forcing you to endure a situation. We must persevere, not tolerate.

Former President Calvin Coolidge put it best when he said;

"Nothing can take the place of persistence.

Talent will not; there is nothing common than unsuccessful men with talent.

Genius will not; unrewarded genius is almost a proverb.

Education will not; the world is full of educated derelicts

Persistence and determination alone are omnipotent."

The importance of persistence can not be overstated. We've been taught this all our lives. We've heard the sayings like; quitters never win and winners never quit; and if at first you don't succeed try, try again.

If we look at Colonel Sanders, the founder of Kentucky Fried Chicken, we see a perfect example of persistence. He attempted different business ventures all his life, finally becoming a success in his senior years. Had he given up at retirement age we never would have known the name of Kentucky Fried Chicken.

We must program our minds to be persistent. We must do this well in advance of the set backs that will surely come. This way when these set backs come we will have already made up our minds to continue past them towards our goals. We must resolve in advance that we will never give up, no matter what happens.

If you wait until you are overwhelmed with problems before you try to develop persistence it will very difficult. You won't have enough time to develop the right attitude. The key then is to develop the persistence attitude in advance of the ups and downs of life. The problems of life can't be avoided, but you can be psychologically prepared.

Power

African Americans need to understand exactly what power is and how it is achieved.

Power is the ability to influence others. This includes economic, sociological, and psychological. Political power is in the hands of whoever controls these three.

There are three types of power structure. Those in power can have one, two or all three types

The first and most simple is coercive power. Simply put, the strongest is in charge. This could be the one with the most guns, biggest army, or something else that the people fear. The coercive leader forces his will on those he leads. More often he is more feared than he is respected. If one person holds this power, he is a dictator. Sometimes it's group or political party, like the Communist Party in China. It can also be an entire race, like the whites that ruled South Africa during Apartheid. This is also the type of power that Europeans had over the African they had enslaved.

Next we have the legitimate power. It is called legitimate because the people accept it. These types of power structures are usually democracies but also include, kings, queens, sultans, etc., which are accepted as legitimate rulers in some countries. It's important to note that all the people might not accept the government. Therefore even a democracy may have to use coercive power at times. A perfect example is the American Civil War.

Finally we have charismatic power. This is when people like the leader because of his personality or some other trait. Many charismatic leaders are also religious figures. The some of the most notable examples are; Moses, Buddha, Jesus Christ, and the prophet of Islam, Muhammad. Their persona was so strong, that religions developed around them and continued on after they left this worldly life.[4]

Sometimes a leader comes along who poses all three of these leadership qualities. For example, Hitler was legitimately elected, loved by many Germans and in the end became a ruthless dictator. There are Neo-Nazis in America who still claim love for him to this day.

As stated earlier, power is the ability to control and influence other people. There are many factors involved in controlling people. For example, coercive power is limited by how vulnerable a person is. Native Americans did not make good slaves, because they weren't vulnerable to many of the things Africans were. First of all the Native Americans had tribal organizations that could be mobilized to go to war against the Europeans. This meant that if they kept them as slaves, there was the possibility of a war party coming to free them. The Africans in America on the other hand had no one to fight for their freedom. Another thing that made the Native Americans less vulnerable was the fact that this country was their home and they could hide out in the wilderness. The only thing the Europeans could do with them was put them on Reservations.

---

[4] The term worldly life is used, hoping not to offend or promote any particular religious belief.

The Africans in Africa were in the same situation, there were too many of them in their native land to make slavery profitable for Europeans in Africa. Instead they chose to live amongst them as conquers. There's a lesson to be learned from this. Black people need to realize, that if they decrease their vulnerability, they decrease the effects of coercive power. For example, if you make it a point to save money, better your education, and always put in résumé's; you are less vulnerable to a boss that abuses you. He might be able to take your job, but you have control over your standard of living. In other words you have more power over your life than he does. Most people in general and African Americans in particular are not in this position.

The purpose of this book is to show you ways to lessen your vulnerability and to give the African Americans the power to control their own destiny as a people.

Chapter 2
Economics

Webster's defines Economics as: a social science concerned chiefly with description and analysis of the production, distribution, and consumption of goods and services.

Freedom is knowledge

As stated earlier, the lock of ignorance is broken with knowledge. To gain true economic freedom, we must acquire the same information as our would be masters. Notice the usage of the word information and not money.

Acquiring lots of money will bring financial freedom to some degree. Still this is not total freedom. Remember there were some slaves, with rich masters, who lived better than some of the poor white people. The fact of the matter is they were still slaves.

The question is then, what is Economic Freedom? Basically, it is the ability to choose the way you earn and spend your money. There are some who would say we are free and we do have choices. Let us take a look at this statement. How often have you heard stories about people who have been turned down for jobs, solely because they were an African American? Maybe it was someone you knew, or it might have even been you; and we don't even have to be reminded of the discrimination that exists in the housing market.

To have choices you most know the options. The reason many would say they have freedom is they don't try to exercise all their options. If you never try to move to an all white area, you never have to admit to yourself that there are places where they don't want you to live.

There are many young African Americans, who don't even know the difference between a checking and savings account. This limits their ability to choose the best type of bank account for their needs. What options do they have if they don't know the choices? Often they will let the bank's representative decide on the type of account that they open. This most often results in them entering into an agreement that is more favorable for the bank.

It is therefore important for African American parents to talk to their children about finances. Remember talk, not complain. In his book "Rich Dad, Poor Dad," Robert T. Kiyosaki mentions that the rich talk to their children about money. He states how the poor dad would not allow the subject of money to be discussed at the dinner table. Whereas the rich dad encouraged this type of talk.

In order to teach our children about finances, we have to learn about finances. An easy way to start would be to read the business section of the local paper. It's not

necessary go out and buy "The Wall Street
"The London Financial Times," even thou
good newspapers. All you have to do is ta
that you usually read, and check out the bus
This way you have access to information at
in or affecting your community.

There is an old saying," if you want v
you must do what we do." Therefore if we
late someone's results we must imitate the

Imitation not Abandonment

We must be careful when we imitate   . It
can have a bad effect on ones self estee   , another cultures way at the expense of you   itating
can be seen as surrendering. To use th   . of the
street, this is called selling out. Often p ———— iis state
will act more like the people they are ..... g than
those people themselves. An African American who
sounds more white that the average white person, or the
gay man who is more feminine than the average woman
are just two examples of this. Think about it, just how
happy can these individuals be with themselves if they
are trying extra hard to be somebody else?

So when it is suggested to imitate, what is meant is,
give the impression of surrendering, to take the usable
qualities of another, and add them to what you already
have. This is progress. It is a gradual betterment, appear-

ing to surrender on the outside, but on the inside remaining strong.

An illustration of this would be the American music and dance scene. African Americans took European instruments, language, and music forms and combined them with African ones and developed whole new music genres. Imitating and adding, not abandoning and forgetting, have led us from the soulful Spirituals to Blues, Jazz, Rhythm and Blues, Rap and Hip Hop. African Americans have established themselves as the leading force in music trends for the last fifty years.

The advances in dance have been just as remarkable. The European dance form of Ballet takes years of formal study and discipline to master. Meanwhile the inner-city housing projects and street corners have produced the art of Beak dancing, which is now recognized art form world wide.

A perfect example of economic imitation without the abandonment would be the Japanese. They took an American invention, the transistor and made it profitable. When Bell Labs first invented the transistor, they had plenty of ideas about what to do with it in the near future. The Japanese on the other hand *immediately* built transistor radios and made lots of money. Americans then developed integrated circuits and computer technologies, but most consumer products that use these technologies are produced in Japan. The Japanese have shown that they will take an American invention and utilize it with innovation, whereas the sellout will follow the lead of those they would like to imitate.

This is not something that the Japanese have just started doing. They have been doing it for over 145 years. Back in 1857 when they felt their independence was threatened by foreign trade, they debated how to defeat the Europeans who threatened them. One of their Ministers, Hotta Masayoshi, wrote a memorandum. In it he said: "I am therefore convinced that our policy should be to conclude friendly alliances, to send ships to foreign countries everywhere and conduct trade, to copy the foreigners where they are at their best and so repair our own shortcomings, to foster our national strength and complete our armaments, and so *gradually* subject the foreigners to our influence until in the end all the countries of the world know the blessings of perfect tranquility and our hegemony (domination) is acknowledged throughout the globe." Basically what he meant was, pretend to accept their superiority over us, learn to use there knowledge to our benefit while at the same time, we slowly infiltrate until we are in control...

We must learn to follow the Japanese example. Our task is not a simple one, but as a people we've overcome many adversities over the past four hundred years, so it can be done. We must utilize new skills, while at the same time holding on to our own cultural values. We must find a balance. Taking in the things that benefit and empower us, and not those that would give our would be masters power over us, while at the same time holding on to the aspects of our own culture that keep us strong.

One of the things we should imitate is the sharing of information. This doesn't mean that you should give away your business secrets, or tell twenty people about the one job opening you are going for. What this refers to is information that won't hurt you, but may help you. For instance, you buy a home using a lender who has special deal for first time minority homebuyers. Many would not share this information with other African Americans. They'd rather stay one step ahead of the Jones'.

They don't realize that, the more African Americans who own homes the better it is for them. First off it gives them more people they can network with to gather information. Who better to get homeowner advice from, than a homeowner? Also as more African Americans buy homes it strengthens the marketability of others. What is meant by this is: A lot of real estate brokers are motivated by prejudice as well as profits. If a lone Black man wants to buy a house, and the broker thinks he may lose five prejudice white costumers behind one sale, that Black man is going be too steered away. He may be the nicest broker in the world. Lose five verses gain one, the one is going to lose, its business, not personal. On the other hand if the broker knows that there are many more potential Black home buyers or the Black man has a few friends or relatives who may also be looking to buy, he may ignore the prejudice and chase the profits. Remember there is strength in numbers.

There is one stumbling block when it comes to imitating others. African Americans still aren't accepted by the society at large. American born whites with young children for example, will try not to buy a house neighbored by at least two Black families. As the number of Black families increase, the chances of a white family with young children moving in decreases. In her book, "Don't believe the hype", Farai Chideya states," In one poll, 73 percent of whites said they would be unwilling to move into a neighborhood that was 36 percent Black. Twenty seven percent of whites said they would be unwilling to move into a neighborhood that was just 8 percent Black."

She also mentions a phenomenon known as "tipping." This is the trend for whites to move out of a neighborhood that has becomes more than 8 percent Black. Therefore if Blacks are 12 percent of the population and whites flee when the percentage reaches 8, integration is therefore impossible.

This doesn't mean that white families will run as soon as the first Black family moves next door, buying and selling houses aren't that easy. It depends on many factors, including how much equity a person has and how fast they can sell their house.

This problem is almost specific to white families with

young children. Young Single whites and those without children have moved into Black neighborhoods in New York City for example. They do this because it's close to where they work or they're looking at a house or co-op as an investment opportunity. The plan is usually to move once they get married or start having children. There are exceptions to this, for instance Hasidic Jews have shown a willingness to live near Blacks of West Indian decent. Part of the reason for this is many other Europeans don't accept them either. Other than this white flight has been the norm.

The fact is, many white Americans moved to the suburbs to get their children away from African Americans. They fear living near African Americans. Even some of the newly arrived immigrants have followed suit. This makes it hard for Blacks to be accepted as equals. To deal with this African Americans must unite and developing their own communities.

Unity

If we are not united to some degree, we won't be able to share information, or anything else for that matter. If you look at certain types of businesses, such as fruit stands, nail salons, convenience stores, etc. You will find that certain types are dominated by certain ethnic groups. This is because of their unity and the fact that they share information. Those who would enslave us, also realize this. They push for our unity or disunity, depending on what benefits them at the time. The main tool they use is the media.

One of the ways they do this is to present African Americans whose opinions are similar to theirs. This does not promote Black unity. A prime example is the news. If you look at the three major cable news channels, you will notice something about the African Americans who appear on these networks. The majority of the African American **men** are political conservatives. Their views on many issues are different than that of most other African Americans. For example, when polls and surveys showed that prior to invading Iraq, the majority of African Americans were against the war, many Blacks in the news media held a different view.

This benefit's the would be enslavers in two ways. First off it gives them a false sense of righteousness on many issues. They can point to these conservative Blacks and say: "Look, this smart, educated, and successful Black man agrees with me." On the other hand it angers many African Americans. They don't agree with many of the Blacks they see in the news media. They therefore become turned off, and don't watch these news channels, because their views are not espoused. This in turn cuts them off from a valuable source of information, and further alienates them from the white society at large.

The second way it helps the would be masters is by silencing the voice of the Blacks whose opinions are different than master's. They simply keep them off the television. Instead, the only Blacks you see are the same ones who say what master wants to hear. This is where the psychological slickness comes into play. There are not many Black reporters supporting major African American grass root issues on a national level, and yet at the same time we can't claim there are no Blacks on the news. So what you end up having is a situation where; lets say African Americans and potential leaders are rallying around and issue like racial quotas for college admissions. Then you have the Black cable news people opposing or at the very least not supporting the view of most other Blacks. This helps to spread the seeds of disunity. This in turn weakens the ability of potential African American leaders to unify the people.

To illustrate this point lets go back to the issue of the Iraqi war. The majority of African Americans opposed the war to topple Sadam Hussein. So did the majority of our leaders. Some of these leaders where on the news almost every day before 9/11. Taking up this cause or that, protesting discrimination or police brutality etc. Now they are silent. Martin Luther King vehemently opposed the Vietnam War. Many Black leaders have made it known that they oppose the war, but they are not shouting it from the mountain tops. They remember what happened to Martin Luther King.

On the other hand there are certain situations when the want us to follow other African Americans, basically when it is profitable for them. They will present African American sports and entertainment figures to our young as role models, and these role models will either explicitly or implicitly tell our children to buy certain products. It doesn't matter that these products are over priced and your money could be better spent else ware; they've sold us the idea that if you want to be in the in crowd, you have to buy such and such athletic shoe or so and so designer jeans.

Some would argue that these companies want white people to buy their products also. The thing these people neglect to add to this argument is white people tend to buy what they can afford and tend to have a little more money than Blacks. African Americans spend a greater percentage of their incomes on clothing than white America. Another argument they may use is there are African Americans companies producing some of these products now. My reply to them is, it doesn't matter who's exploiting the Black community, over priced clothing is not what African Americans need right now.

There's another problem with these role models. The fact that the majority of them are athletes and entertainers is not good. It's not that these are bad careers, in fact if you have talent, it is strongly suggested that **you** exploit it. What's troubling is the majority of the role models they push at us make their living entertaining white people. It is shameful that when most young African American men think of becoming millionaires, they think in terms of singing, rapping or running in touch downs for the amusement of white people; or selling drugs to Black people.

White people also love their athletes, entertainers, and even their gangsters, but when it's time for role models they look towards, President Bush, Bill Gates, Warren Buffet and the like. Their role models own the teams that our role models play for.

What Black people need is a change of mind. Instead of aspiring to play on the team, African Americans should be trying to own it. They need to believe that they can own it.

Attitude

✗ The author was once told a story that showed how a mind-set could influence your reality. There was this man on a business trip in Atlanta. Upon arriving at the airport he entered a taxi cab. He noticed the cab driver had a Jamaican accent. He asked the driver if he was from Jamaica. The driver replied that he was. The business man then told the driver that he loved vacationing in Jamaica, and that he thought it was a beautiful country. The driver thanked him for the compliment.

A little while later the cab driver said to the business man, "I have my own business."

"What?" the business man replied.

"I have my own business," the cab driver restated.

"This cab is my business, and once I save up enough money I'm going to buy another taxi and hire someone to drive it for me."

"That's good," the business man said.

This made the business man think. You have people who are born in the United States, who complain about racism and the lack of jobs, and here you have this Black immigrant who has established his own business and is already planning expansion.

What is the difference between this Jamaican immigrant and the average unemployed African American? Attitude!

It is important that we understand this. At the time this was written the New York Amsterdam News ran a headline that read "48% UNEMPLOYED, Almost half of New York's Black male population is jobless."[5]

High unemployment rates don't stop immigration to the U.S. This is because the United States has high rate of opportunity.

If you think you can, probably you can; but if you think you can't, you definitely can't. We have to believe that we can do whatever anyone else can do. The United States truly is the land of opportunity. African Americans just have to look and work harder.

There's a common myth in the African American community, that foreigners are entitled to financial assis-

---

[5] Vol.95 No. 9 February 26-March 3, 2004

tance, just because they are from another country. The truth is they often take advantage of small business loans and other programs that could be of advantage to African Americans.

In fact many of the civil rights laws that these people take for granted, were originally passed basically for the benefit of African Americans. We must ask our selves, why is it that many if not most African Americans aren't utilizing these opportunities? The answer is lack of knowledge.

Acquire

We must acquire information. You should make a commitment to yourself to life long learning. Knowledge is power. This is what separates the top dog from the rest of the pack. The more knowledgeable someone is in their profession, the better the services they are able to provide. The author's experience with a couple of dentist illustrates this point. Two different dentists informed him that he had a major case of gum disease and that oral surgery was needed. Fortunately he procrastinated. You see the author also suffers from Hypertension. He happened to be doing some research on the medicine he was using to treat his Hypertension, Procardia XL. It just so happens that this medication causes the gums to swell. The dentists were informed that he was on this medication, but apparently did not know about this particular side effect. When the author stopped taking this medication the swelling subsided. Therefore they were actually misdiagnosing the problem. The result could have been painful treatments that would not have eased the swelling, and a possible malpractice suite.

Reading is important. It is to the mind like exercise is to the body. What to read? Well if you are looking for economic and financial freedom, you should read things that contain this type of knowledge. We must read books, websites and yes the business section of the daily paper. Otherwise we will continuously be left behind, because there is so much we don't know. For instance most African Americans don't know about the United States Small Business Administration. This organization offers assistance to small businesses.

One form of assistance that they offer is the guarantee of loans under section 7(a) of the Small Business Act. This is similar to an FHA loan. The only difference is the money is used for a business instead of a home. If you are interested in a Small Business Administration backed loan, you must first find a lender. Most banks will offer this type of loan. They usually do this if they feel that the application has some weakness. They might feel that the applicant might be a slight credit risk. The money is actually being loaned by the bank, but the Small Business

Administration guarantees to pay back all or a part of the loan if the borrower fails to pay. You must qualify for an SBA loan.

In order to get a 7(a) loan, the applicant must first be eligible. Repayment ability from the cash flow of the business is a primary consideration in the SBA loan decision process but good character, management capability, collateral, and owner's equity contribution are also important considerations. All owners of 20 percent or more are required to personally guarantee SBA loans.

Many will read this and think that you need an MBA or some other college degree to be eligible for this type of loan. This is not a necessity. What you basically need is a solid business plan. If you can convince others that your plan is viable and well thought out and you are some what of a good credit risk you can probably convince some banker to provide you with a SBA loan. There are plenty of banks, many of them African American owned that claimed to be community orientated, it's up to you to make an effort to make them prove it.

The thing that stops most African Americans from trying is they've started to believe the myth; African Americans are not intelligent and business minded enough to run a profitable business.

If we look at the evidence this myth is proved false. There are thousands of Black owned businesses in the U.S. Ranging in everything from steel production to Black hair care products manufacture; from savings banks to investment banking. The list goes on; there are funeral parlors, barbershops, accountants and computer software developers. In fact practically every business that whites engage in, you can find at least one Black owned firm doing the same business.

There are other examples that we are not so proud of, yet show the genius and entrepreneurial spirit of our people. It is the selling of illicit street drugs. Don't get it wrong, drugs hurt our community and, drug dealers have done more harm than the KKK could ever hope to. Still we have to admit that some of these gangs are highly organized. There was one gang in New York City that had over three hundred employees. These people had shifts and reported to supervisors. This was an organization run buy a kid from the projects. There are people in business schools right now working on their MBA's, learning the skills this kid showed naturally. The message that we need to impart to our youth is if you're good at selling crack, you'd probably be good at selling cars.

Historically we also have a tradition as business men. For instance in West Africa there was a growth of trade across the Sahara that started to flourish about the year 1000. Trade routes were established from western Africa across the Sahara to North Africa, the Middle East, and Europe to the north. Gold and Kola nuts were the main exports from western Africa. The kingdoms and empires at the southern edge of the Sahara became wealthy by controlling this trade. Ghana was one of the first great kingdoms to be established in West Africa. It was probably started around the year 300 A.D. It reached it's height around the year 1000 A.D. During the 1200's Mali replaced Ghana as the dominant kingdom in West Africa. The Songhai Empire eventually replaced Mali as the leading power in West Africa around the 1500's. It must be pointed out the Songhai at its peak had an army of over 20,000 men.

The wealth of these trade states is best exemplified by the story of Mansa Musa. He ruled Mali 1312 to about 1337. In 1324 he made Hajj to the Islamic Holy city of Mecca. His party included thousands of people and hundreds of camels carrying gold and other items of value. He and his party spent and gave away so much gold, in cities like Mecca and others where they stopped, that for a few years gold lost much of it's value in these areas, in some places you practically couldn't even give it away. It can be argued, that he was one of the richest, if not the richest man in the world at this time.

Maintenance

This shows that our lack of economic power is not because of a disability. Rather it is because we've been taught to maintain a particular mind set. This mindset consists of a set of principles that prevent the acquisition and maintenance of wealth. The author remembers as a child, growing up in the Bronx, this attitude very well. He recalls one incident in particular. He and a group of friends were 'hanging on the corner' talking about jobs and money. The author expressed his desire to become a millionaire. One of his friends commented that the author lived in a dream world, and he need to snap out of it. The friend went on to say; he knew as a Black man he'd never be a millionaire and he wasn't going to fool himself. As long as the friend thought like this, he was right; he'd never be a millionaire. I call this type of friend a dream killer. First he kills his own dreams then he works on yours. This type of person should be avoided at all cost. It comes down to role models and peer pressure. Just like when a good parent tells their children to stay away from certain people, we should do the same as adults. If you are a law abiding person you probably stay away from criminals in general, but keep company with the dream killers. Later on it will be discussed how to detect and avoid these type of people. Remember positive thinking doesn't all ways work, but negative thinking never does.

This brings to mind Jesse Jackson's famous line: 'keep hope alive'. To have hope, is to dream of a favorable outcome. We must maintain the dream. The majority of the players in the NBA dreamed of becoming professional basketball players while still in high school. They worked at accomplishing this dream until it became a reality. The rest of us might have fantasized about playing in Madison Square Garden, but we told our selves it was just that, a fantasy. The dream killers would say, 'you **have** to be over six feet and have special physical abilities to play in the pro's. On the contrary, Spud Webb and Mugsy Bogues prove that as long as you have the dream and desire and are willing to work at it, practically anything is possible. If you put your mind to it you have the power to do or be practically anything you want. Like the little train engine that could, you have to tell your self: yes I can.

✳ Another problem that African Americans have is the consumer mind set. When most African American think of accomplishing goals, what they are actually thinking about is acquiring consumer goods. While other groups dream of selling us these goods. This can be explained by two old jokes:

Joke 1, a Genie is released from a bottle by three men. A Black man, a white Anglo Saxon man, and a Jewish man. The Genie grants each man one wish. The Anglo Saxon man wishes for Stocks, bonds, and some Real-estate. The Black man wishes for a few million dollars. Finally the Jewish man wishes for some fake gold chains and the Black man's address.

Joke 2, if a Black man wins the lotto he buys a Cadillac. If a Jew wins the lotto he opens a store and with the profits he buys two Cadillacs.

White people will find these jokes funny. Most African Americans don't, the truth hurts. This puts us in a situation where others profit from our dreams. This is not an accident. Think about it, if a group of people had a dream, and their dream paid you money, would you want to stop their dream. Probably not. Now on the other hand, if their dream took money out of your pocket, you would try to stop it? Probably yes.

We are following a pattern that started in Africa. The Europeans came to Africa selling guns and trinkets, basically consumer items. They traded these for slaves and raw materials. These were capital goods, they could be used later to produce more wealth. The Africans on the other hand ended up with a lot of trinkets and no wealth.

African Americans need to develop a producer mind set. Instead of trying to buy Cadillacs and gold chains, we need to dream of making and selling them. If we are to ever get ahead as a people we need to develop this mind set. As I mentioned earlier many drug dealers have this mind set, so do many of the behind the scenes people in the record industry. This mind set is something we all need to bring into our personal lives.

This is not to say you shouldn't want the finer things in life. It's just that more balance is needed. It's sort of like the old saying; "Champagne thoughts with beer money." Examples of this are seen in the work place. There will be Black and white co-workers who earn approximately the same amount; yet the Black one will have a nicer car, more expensive jewelry, and fancier clothes. The white worker on the other hand has the larger bank account. He may have money in the stock market, mutual funds or some type of individual retirement plan. Herein our problem lies, our money is on our backs. If they were both laid off, the Black man will be the nicest dressed person in the unemployment office. Whereas the white one will be the one with enough money saved to hold him for a few months.

The rich have always understood it's not how much money you make that makes you rich; it's how much you keep. A perfect example would be MC Hammer. One of his albums was the best selling rap album of it's time. His concerts were sold out nation wide. He was making money hand over fist. He was also spending it as fast as he was making it. As soon as the hit records stopped, he was bankrupt. He fell victim to the same trap that many other African Americans fall into; pretending to be richer than they really are. This is an expensive trap, which basically is designed to keep you poor. This trap is easy to avoid, simply don't buy what you can't afford. This includes credit card use. The rich carry credit cards so they don't have to carry cash. They usually have the ability to pay their entire bill when it is due. Whereas the poor, (this includes most Blacks) carry them so they can purchase things they can't really afford. When the bill is due they can usually only afford the minimum due payment. You generally can not get a head by getting into debt. There are some exceptions, borrowing money to purchase a house or business are examples.

Buying a house is one of the best ways to accumulate wealth and financial freedom. This is not to say that a house will make you rich, but generally in the long run, home owners end up better off than renters. Probably the most talked about benefit are the tax breaks. Another potential benefit is fixed mortgages usually don't go up, whereas rents do. There is another benefit that's seldom mentioned. When you purchase a house it's yours. You own it, if there's a tree on your property, it's your tree, that's in your ground, it belongs to you. There is a sense of pride and freedom that comes with home ownership. Also you are now free from renter's prison. No more landlords telling you what you can and can not do, or have in your place of residence. In order to own a home though you must be able to save.

Another way to accumulate wealth is to pay yourself first. Take ten percent of your pay check and put it in the bank. This is not to be a rainy day savings, because it will rain a lot. This money should be used for only three things; One, to purchase a home or business; two, if you lose your job or are unable to work **AND** unemployment or disability has run out; and three, the most important to fund your retirement. This is very important for your economic and financial freedom. Being able to retire and not work is a luxury you can afford, if you start saving for it now.

Awareness

We must be aware; there are many who have a vested interest in keeping African Americans down. There are different groups, which have as many different reasons that we stay in our place. We will examine three of them.

First we have the Ignorant Racist. Often times they will consider their own appearance and behavior as normal and therefore desirable. This type of individual often doesn't know much about the group he hates, and that is basically why he hates them. He usually gets his information from other racist, and therefore much of his opinion is given to him by someone else. The author met this type of person as a young adult, while traveling to Minnesota. The individual informed the author he didn't like Jews. When the author asked him how many Jews he knew, the individual said he had never actually met a Jewish person. This individual was told certain things about Jews, and believed them. If someone is taught from early on that Blacks lack intelligence, they will carry this belief with them often times in spite of evidence to the contrary. This person will try to keep Blacks down because he believes they should be kept down. He will have a problem with the way other groups look, behave and often dress. This is the police officer who pulls over

Blacks because he believes most Black youth are criminals, this is the landlord who doesn't want Blacks in his building because he believes that Blacks will tear it up, not pay their rent, and chase away the good white people. This is the employer who doesn't want to hire Blacks because he believes, they are lazy, they will steal (more about this later), and white customers will be turned off by them, causing him to loose business. It must be kept in mind that beliefs are hard to change. People who are Democrats, when they are poor, may often times vote Republican if they become well off, but they usually don't change deeply held beliefs about, religion, race, and right and wrong. Therefore this type of racist often won't change his beliefs. The key to stopping this type of racism is to stop it before it starts. This is done by educating children before their minds are corrupted.

Next we have the Scared Racist. Part of his fear, (it seems that this type is most often male) is based on the belief system of the ignorant racist, and part is based on low self esteem. They often fear loosing jobs or prestige to African Americans. They often think to themselves, how smart can I be if I have the same job as an African American. Often times this type of racist won't even take a job if he knows that he may be working with many Blacks and may be under the supervision of African Americans. This explains why many whites wouldn't take many civil service jobs in certain urban areas during the 70's and 80's. This trend though, has been reversing itself for about ten years or so, because many of the blue collar and lower level white collar jobs are being lost to overseas companies. This in turn is forcing many whites to reconsider these urban based civil service jobs that had given up on only two decades ago. Another very important issue for the scared racist is sex. The root cause of the majority of Lynching of Black men in the United States has been for some form of sexual contact with white women. This issue will be discussed in greater detail in the following chapter. The scared racist will often change his beliefs if he gets exposure to other groups and his fears aren't turned into realities. The problem with that is African Americans will often act in stereotypical ways, reinforcing those fears.

The final type of racist we will discus is the Head Racist in Charge. This type of individual may have some of the character traits of both the Ignorant and Scared Racist, but those traits are not what motivate him. This type of racist usually has economic or some type of political power. He uses the discriminated group as a scapegoat. He unites the people with hatred, which is a strong emotional force. He rises to power, or stays in power, by uniting the people against their 'common' enemy. The people become so involved in hating the enemy, they fail to realize that the leader is using them as well. A perfect example would be Adolph Hitler, who ruled Germany during the 1930's and 40's. Often times this person doesn't care about either group, his real motivation is personal power or gain.

Sometimes the Head Racist in Charge will abuse a particular race because he knows that they can't defend themselves. It doesn't matter what race the victim is as long as he is not part of the dominant group and the head racist can achieve a particular goal. An example of this was the Tuskegee Syphilis experiment. This was an experiment in which a number of African Americans who had contracted Syphilis where purposely not cured. The white doctors in charge needed to know what would happen if Syphilis were left untreated. It really didn't matter who the victims were, but the doctors knew that if the had done this experiment on whites they might have had problems. It should be noted, that this experiment went on from 1932 until 1972. The experiment was stopped when news of it reached the general public, and it proved to be an embarrassment for the U.S. government.

The Head Racist in Charge often uses institutional racism. They will zone schools, set hospital billing policies and banking procedures to discriminate against poor people in general, and Blacks specifically. For example lets take a look at traditional mortgage requirements.

- No home loans for less than $50,000.
- A clean credit history and at least four accounts at banks or retail merchants.
- Two years steady work at the same job.

- No "mattress money" (cash for a down payment must come from a verifiable, approved source, e.g. a bank savings account).
- No loans in neighborhoods where more than 40 percent of the homes are occupied by renters (as opposed to homeowners).
- Monthly mortgage payments shall not exceed 28 percent of gross monthly earnings.

At first glance these requirements don't look discriminatory. They don't blatantly discriminate against African Americans. Yet statistics show that these rules affect Blacks to a higher degree than whites. Economics are changing some of these rules though; many banks can no longer afford to exclude Blacks from the home buying process.

Defense

The two main weapons we have against the Head Racist in Charge are exposure and unity.

A prime example of exposure stopping the Head Racist in Charge is the Tuskegee experiment. Once news of it hit the general public, the experiment was allegedly stopped. Another example, though not so obvious, is that of Malik Shabazz (Malcolm X). He threatened to bring the United States up on charges before the International

Court. This might have proved to be a major embarrassment for the U.S., who was fighting the Vietnam War, 'defending the world' against communism and preaching democracy; yet many of it's own citizens could not vote. As far as the racist elements of the U.S. government were concerned his (Malcolm X) death could not have been timelier. The problem with exposure is African Americans lack control and access to the media.

Unity is much more effective, though just as hard to obtain and maintain. The effectiveness of this was best illustrated by Martin Luther King and his freedom marches. Whereas his death exposed the difficulty in maintaining unity. The movement often dies with its leader. If the leader isn't killed he is often discredited.

To recap, Blacks must remember; when intuitional racism is encountered it must be exposed. The more people that know about it, the harder it is for the Head Racist in Charge to continue his practices; and on the other hand we must become united in our stand against institutional racism. United we stand, divided we fall.

Remember another aspect of the unity and exposure tactic is economics. Business' tend to think in terms of; will the institution make money or loose it with exposure or the financial might of unity? The threat of losing or the promise of gaining a lot of money can change most people's opinions about a lot of things.

Economic Power

Money is power. We have heard this statement so many times; no one should doubt its truthfulness. More accurately money is a powerful tool. African Americans must learn to use this tool. For the most part they have been taught to work for money, instead of allowing money to work for them.

African Americans need to realize that; a considerable proportion of high income earners get their monies from investments. The higher the income, the bigger the part investment plays.

Basically, investing is spending money on something that hopefully will pay more money later. In the United States there are seven major types of investments. They are (1) savings accounts, (2) life insurance, (3) business investments, (4) real estate, (5) bonds, (6) stocks, and (7) mutual funds.

Care must be taken not to become too obsessed with money. Greed weakens the human spirit. The greedy man is the con artist's best friend. Thinking they will get something for nothing blinds them to the fact, that they are actually giving up something for nothing. This capitalist society is built on greed. African Americans must learn to recognize the greedy and be patient in their dealings with them. Wait before you buy and spend. Let them become desperate. The longer you hold on to your money the more they will give you for it. For example, if you apartment building is not up to par, organize a rent strike. Watch how fast the cheapest land lord fixes things when his bread and butter are threatened.

We must learn to judge things by how much they cost, not just in money but also in time. Time is more valuable than money. Money lost can be regained but time lost is gone forever. Still we mustn't become obsessively cheap either. You can end up wasting valuable time hunting down so called bargains. Only to discover that your bargain is actually a piece of junk, that will soon need replacing. You may save some money, but the real cost may be time and piece of mind.

The same thing goes for cutting corners and freebies. Remember nothing worth having comes easy. Think about this. If you are always trying to get out of work or cutting corners, what is the real cost. The odds are you will be passed up for promotions. If you are promoted many co workers won't have respect for you.

As far as freebies go, there are none. Nothing is for free. Everything has a cost. When someone gives away a so called freebie, there is something in it for them. Most drug addicts will tell you the first time they used drugs, they were free. Look at the price they paid for this freebie. Even if a person is giving to charity, there is almost always something in it for him. At the very least the giver of charity will receive a good feeling in the heart or a cleared conscience.

Then there is the other side. People often become dependant on charity. If someone gives enough charity, they have some control over the receiver of it. Ask any one who's ever been on public assistance or a Methadone maintenance plan. Warning, avoid the free ride.

Chapter 3
Sociological

Webster defines Sociology as the science of society, social institutions, and social relationships.

Morals

One of the major issues affecting the African American community is crime. Crime is a moral problem as well as a social one. At this time it is the most pressing problem facing African Americans in general and our youth in particular. It is the reason most whites are afraid to live around Blacks; and it is one of the main reasons many middle class African Americans have fled the inner cities.

Most of our social, economic, and psychological based actions are based on two emotions; greed and fear.

We go for what we want because of greed or to a lesser degree, desire. We try to get love, relationships, promotions, better homes nicer cars etc. The average human will never say, I've made enough money, let me stop earning." The prophet of Islam, Muhammad said; "The only thing that fills the belly of man is dirt." What he meant by this is the dirt of the grave, in other words, death is the only thing that prevents man from wanting more.

On the opposite end, our fear of some type of punishment or shame prevents us from doing some other things. Some don't steal because they fear going to jail. Some won't use drugs because they fear the consequences of addiction. We strive for relationships because we fear loneliness. The list goes on.

For a society to be stable, fear and greed need to be in some sort of balance. This is not the case with many in today's African American society. We have allowed greed to overtake our fears. Many will do anything for money or pleasure. They don't even think twice about the consequences of their actions.

In fact it has become popular to be a criminal (thug). Many African American males are actually trying to look like thugs, even when they are not. It has gotten so bad in the music industry that many claim to be and try to live their lives as if they really are thugs. They express these attitudes in their rap lyrics and music videos. Whereas white performers make gangster movies, yet they are rarely ever involved in this in real life. We must remember that music is an integral part of our culture. Long after we forget the quotes and sayings of famous people, we will remember our favorite song lyrics. If our children sing I'm a pimp long enough, it is going to have some kind of effect on their psyche.

This brings up another very controversial subject,

bringing young children on jail visits. This has become very popular among African Americans. Psychologists have discovered that this is not a good thing for our youth.

First of all, because of the way prison guards and officials tend to treat visitors. They don't treat them well, and this causes resentments in the parent/guardian as well as in the child. This can teach a child to resent instead of respect the law enforcement community.

Second, jail becomes a less scary and more socially acceptable place. The more often a child or an adult for that matter visit's a correctional facility, the more comfortable they tend to become with that type of setting. This can teach children that it's not that scary to go to prison.

A third reason is if children are constantly exposed to this type of environment, they tend to think that the behavior of the inmates is normal social behavior. They often tend to see the inmates as people 'who keep it real.'

If our children are constantly taught that a criminal life is acceptable, we are almost guaranteeing them a lifestyle filled with jails and early death. Remember when we discussed imitation and not abandonment. Many of our youth have chosen to imitate gangsters. You will often hear rap lyrics praising or eluding to the likes of John Gotti or "Sammy the Bull" Gravano. It seems like that they not only want to be gangsters, but they want to be white gangsters. We don't hear many of youth saying they want to be the President of the United States or of some major corporation. It as if many in the Black community have lost a sense of the difference between right or wrong. What is needed is a spiritual reawakening of Black society. Blacks should understand to grow spiritually one must grow morally.

There are many reasons for this predicament, but the primary one is, this is the way Master wants it. It serves him on two social fronts, economical and political.

Social-Economic

As long as Blacks are fighting, killing, and robbing from each other, Master doesn't have to worry about us trying to change our status or take his jobs. He can sell you a gold chain for a $100. Then another man can steal it from you and sell it to a pawnshop for let's say $50. The people who benefit are the original seller, the pawnshop and the thief. The law abiding citizen is out of $100, and has nothing to show for it. He ends up trying to replace what was stolen. Thus the rich get richer and the poor get poorer. It also motivates the thief to continue stealing.

An additional problem is, many African Americans have little faith in the criminal justice system and are reluctant to call the police when a crime has been committed. Among our youth it's an epidemic. They see going to the police as snitching.

The way of the street is to take the law into your own hands. When this happens, the original victim often ends up getting arrested. He then ends up watching the original perpetrator go free. This in turn lowers people's faith in the legal system even more.

Social-Political

The other way it serves Master is on the social political front. First off, many young Black males now have criminal records and can't vote, run for office, or serve jury duty. This is profound because political change often comes from the youth. If our youth are disenfranchised, it becomes hard for us to change the status quo.

Running away from it doesn't help either. We should also be advised that moving out of Black neighborhoods also cancels out the African American vote. In predominately white areas, the elected officials are usually white. This practically guarantees that Blacks living in these areas will not have many Black officials representing them. They will often have no one who can identify with what they are going through if he/she is the victim of racism, and if you live in a predominately white community you probably will be the victim of some type of racism sooner or later.

It also weakens the vote in the Black area that they moved from. This can bee seen in Harlem, a section of New York City. The African American middle class started abandoning this traditional Black neighborhood many years ago. Thus leaving the area in the hands of a small group of citizens.

For example if you attend a typical community board meeting in Harlem you are apt to see many whites in attendance.

Community Boards are local representative bodies with a formal role designated by the City Charter in such matters as land use, determining local budget priorities, and monitoring City service delivery. Each board consists of up to 50 unsalaried members appointed by the Borough President from among active, involved people of each community. Community Boards serve as advocacy organizations for new programs and facilities needed in their respective districts.

It is interesting to note that in a traditionally African American community, whites who often don't live in the area and have not been elected, have some say over how the community is run. This is because the African Americans who might be willing to hold these positions are trying to get away from the area instead of improving it.

There's also the fiasco called the jury system. As stated before, many of our youth have criminal records and therefore can not serve jury duty. When a Black man is on trial or being sued and he looks into the jury box, he does not see a jury of his peers. This is just a small part of a larger pattern that has existed since the founding of this country.

One of the biggest parts of this pattern is the Electoral College. This is the complicated system that the United States uses to elect it's President. Each state has a certain amount of Electors, who actually vote for the President and Vice President. This system is used, instead of actually counting the people's vote.

It was because of this system that George W. Bush who lost the popular vote was still able to claim victory.

This system was devised so as to give the slave states political power based on the number of slaves they held. Each state has a certain amount of Electoral votes, based on it's population. Slaves were included in this population.

Every five slaves were counted as three people. In other words a Black man was 3/5 of a white man.

This type of census taking gave the slave states the power of the Black vote, without actually letting the Blacks vote. In effect, if a slave owner had five hundred slaves, it gave him three hundred and one votes.

During Jim Crow it gave the whites in the south even more power. African Americans were counted as whole people, yet they were denied the right to vote. This increased the number of Electoral votes for southern states, yet only the whites had the ability to vote.

In fact it's ironic, that Constitutionally, African American men in the south had gained the *right* to vote fifty years before white American women. Yet white American women were actually voting almost fifty years before the passing of the Voting Rights Act of 1965.

Another link in the in the social chain of slavery is the fact that Blacks usually vote Democrat. This means that any person who runs in a general election as a Democratic Party candidate gets the Black vote, regardless of what he stands for.

It's ironic that the Democratic Party ruled the south for many years after slavery and also opposed equal rights for African Americans.

Former Senator Strom Thurmond strongly opposed the 1957 civil rights bill. During this time he was a Democrat. In fact he was a Democrat from 1929 until 1964. It seems he left the party just before southern Blacks started joining it.

The segregated south was ruled by the Democratic Party. It was President Abraham Lincoln and the Republican Party that incongruously freed the slaves. In 1957 Republican President Dwight D. Eisenhower sent the101st Airborne Division to little Rock Arkansas; thus enabling nine Blacks to integrate Central High.

On the other hand Democratic President Franklin D. Roosevelt started welfare because the Depression put many whites out of work. The Social Security Act that he signed into law, excluded farmers and domestics, which was 65% of the Black labor force. In 1996 another Democrat, Bill Clinton, changed welfare because white taxpayers were tired of paying for it.

In fact since Abraham Lincoln's Presidency we have

had only nine Democratic Presidents. Six of them were from the south. The last two being Jimmy Carter from Georgia and Bill Clinton from Arkansas. It's no secret that in these two states there are certain areas that are still highly segregated. It's also appears, that many bigoted voters supported these candidates. In other words, the Klan sometimes votes Democrat sometimes Republican. They cast their vote for the candidate that supports their issues. Whereas African Americans vote for any Democrat that is running for office, regardless of what he stands for. Can you name one thing President Bill Clinton actually did for African Americans?

This is not to say that Clinton didn't help African Americans; it just underscores the fact that he didn't do anything spectacular for them. In fact his welfare reforms pushed many African Americans off of welfare and into jobs that paid less than they were getting while on welfare.

What's interesting is that, the two Presidents who did the most for African Americans, Lincoln and Kennedy were both assassinated.

There are two other problems that come with constantly voting Democrat.

The first problem is complacency. The Democratic politicians know they can count on the Black vote whether they do for them or not. As stated before, Clinton didn't do much for African Americans, yet they voted to reelect him; Why? Because he's a Democrat. As long as we are predictable, politicians will not be forced to earn our vote. If African Americans learn to switch their votes strategically, both parties will become dependant on them and will cater more to there needs.

The second problem with always voting Democrat is those who want to keep Blacks enslaved know what they are going to do. If your enemy knows you next move, he can devise a strategy to thwart you.

Ironically there is one situation when whites consider Blacks equal citizens. When it's time for war. In every one of this nation's wars African Americans have been *allowed* to fight. African Americans fought for democracy in the Korean War, then, they returned to America and had to ride the back of the bus in Alabama.

Leadership

Every so often a Black leader comes along and preaches for a massive social change. If this leader becomes too popular and develops a large African American following, they are usually killed or discredited. Let's take a look at some of the greatest Black leaders of the 20th century. Martin Luther King and Malcolm X, were assassinated. The controversy over who pulled the triggers in both homicides continues to this day. Marcus Garvey and Elijah Muhammad were both discredited. Garvey for mail fraud and Muhammad for adultery. It is interesting to note that Garvey was pardoned by then

President Calvin Coolidge and then deported. It's almost as if they were scared to kill him, lest he become a martyr, so they sent him into exile.

You may not agree that all or any on this list was a great Black leader. This doesn't change the fact that they each had a large following that stretched nation wide. That's what scares white America. A united Black America, whose leader they can't control.

Envy

One of the major roots of our current situation is envy. (Player hating, to use the parlance of the street.)

Here is a perfect example from when the author was about twelve years old. He was hanging on a Bronx corner with about six other Black men. Their ages ranged from 11 to about 25. One of the men suggested they buy some beer. Someone suggested that they buy it from a new Black owned store that was across the street. The oldest man in the group balked at that idea saying, "I ain't gonna pay that niggers mortgage."

Needless to say they bought the beer from Irving, the Jewish merchant. Irving ended up selling his store to a Latino, whereas the Black owned store ended up going out of business.

This is not to say that Blacks don't support African American businesses. It's just to point out that many African Americans are envious and won't support their own.

Don't tell people all your plans. Remember people are by nature selfish, jealous and envious. If you're praying for a particular job, you are also praying indirectly that someone else doesn't get it.

This extends to violence also. Most African Americans who grew up in the "Hood' know of someone who was killed because of jealousy/envy.

What is the cure for this ailment? It's very simple, GRATITUDE. If you are grateful for what you have, you will not covet what your neighbor has. The best way to develop gratitude is through religion. This includes all religions. It's important to note at this time that second and third generation African American Muslims are facing basically the same problems as Black Christians. We should be aware of the fact that as Black religious service attendance has declined; the very problems we are discussing have risen.

Not only do religious institutions teach and develop gratitude, they also teach other morals and values. They help to give our youth a conscience. This is not to say that attendance to religious services guarantees that a child will grow into a law abiding citizen. However he has a better chance of learning morals in the church or mosque than he does on the street.

The subject of religion brings us to another important issue, the Middle East. Three major religions were born in this area, Christianity, Judaism, and Islam.

Do you know why this area is called the Middle East?

Basically, because the Europeans did not want to call the birth place of "their" religion Africa. Let's take a closer look at this. No one denies that Egypt is in Africa. Egypt is the western neighbor of Israel/Palestine. The only things that separate the two countries are a line drawn on a map and a man made canal. When geography is taught to children, they often have a hard time "understanding" why the so called Middle East is not part of Africa. The only reason adults "understand" it is because they have been told that's the way it is, and they accept this as fact. Why it is not called South Western Asia? In fact Somalia and parts of Ethiopia are further east than Jerusalem. Many scholars now believe Jesus spent much of his early life in Egypt (Africa). Is it coincidence that this time period of his life is missing from the Bible?

Self-preservation

It is interesting to note that as Black on Black crime increased, lynching decreased. There were 3300 reported lynching of African Americans in the United States from 1882 to 1968. This epidemic of Black on Black crime started in the late sixties, when the lynching stopped. Do you see the correlation?

A Klansman said it best when he explained why the

lynching stopped, "we now let the niggers handle our dirty work."

The vast majority of lynching victims in the United States were African American men. African American women were also lynched, for example Laura Nelson in Okemah, Oklahoma. She was murdered on the 5th of May, 1911. Her only crime was she lied to protect her son, who was also lynched. The author knows of no case of a white woman being lynched in the United States. This is not to say there have been any, but that they have not been brought to our attention.

According to the extremely graphic internet website *www.musarium.com/withoutsanctuary/main.html*; there was at least one lynching of a Black man by a Black mob in Florida. This was for the assault of a young African American girl.

Other than that, the primary reason for lynching in the United States has been for some type of assault against a white person, especially against white women. African American males have been lynched for whistling, bumping into, and even looking at white women. This doesn't even include actual rapes robberies and murders. These statements show that white Americans will unite to defend themselves from African Americans. It is now time for African Americans to unite for their own defense. This is not to suggest mob violence. Instead it should serve as a reminder that we should join together to fight all the social ills that are attacking our communities.

We've learned to come together to protest the killing of an unarmed youth by the police. Still if that same unarmed youth is shot down by another Black youth, no one organizes a protest march. Many African Americans were willing to suffer physical harm, even death for the right to vote; but won't risk anything· to make their neighborhood safe for their children.

We are afraid to take certain risk. Fear is the absence of faith. It is no coincidence that many of great leaders were also religious leaders. This brings us back to an earlier statement, "that as Black religious service attendance has declined; the very problems we are discussing have risen." Many now have the attitude, "I only worry about what goes on with my family and household."

This is the wrong attitude to take. Remember your actions or inactions help shape the world your children will inherit. There was a time in the Black community, that if a neighbor saw a child doing wrong that neighbor could chastise the child. Sometimes this even included corporal punishment. The parents even welcomed it. In most urban Black communities this is no longer the case.

If you don't fight for justice now, in time, your children will accept injustice as normal; if you don't fight for law and order now, in time, they will accept lawlessness as normal. Is this what we wish for our children?

This doesn't mean that you must lead a protest march or confront the neighborhood drug dealer. What must be done is that we teach our children morals. This can be done in many ways.

Two of the best ways are;

One, practice them yourself. Try to live your life so that when your children think of good moral behavior, they think of you.

Two, involve them in intuitions that promote these morals. This includes houses of worship, churches, masajid (mosque), synagogues, and temples. It also includes the Boy and Girl Scouts, the YMCA and the YWCA; also included on this list are organized team sports and general family outings.

Following these examples does not guarantee success, but it gives you something to help fight the lure of the street.

Self love

One of the main draw backs to changing our attitude is the way we see ourselves. African Americans have been subjected to mental oppression for so long; it has left a long and deep psychological scar on them. Except for the last forty or so years, Blacks have generally used European concepts to define human beauty.

It can be seen in such innovations as the 'perm' or straitening comb. Many Black women will tell you this makes their hair more manageable. These women will often say their hair looks nicer when it's permed. This statement is under scored by the fact that most Blacks define good hair as strait or curly hair. This doesn't mean that African American women should not perm or straiten their hair. People should have the option to beautify themselves in any way that pleases them. Still it is no coincidence that what African Americans call nice hair, is hair that is similar to that of white people. This attitude can also be seen in Black America's obsession with skin complexion. Though not as prevalent as in the past, many African Americans consider light skin Blacks more attractive than darker skin ones.

This does not mean that people can't choose what looks beautiful to them. It just points out how the European model has defined our concept of beauty. Our concepts of beauty should be based on our looks. Whether it is dark skin, or light skin, thin lips, or thick lips, small behinds or big behinds; our standard should be based on our people. This should apply to other aspects of our culture.

The author's grandmother once said to him, "if white people don't buy it, I don't want it." This attitude is typical of many middle class African Americans. Most don't even realize they think this way.

The early history of Rap music illustrates this point. The Sugar Hill Gang was the first nationwide commercially successful rap group. While appearing on Soul Train, they were interviewed by its host Don Cornelius. After asking them a few questions, he laughed and

asked, "So what do you guys really do for a living."
In other words he was saying he did not recognize
them as successful recording artist. In spite of the fact
that they had a top ten hit that became a gold record.
Many African Americans felt this way about Rap music.
It wasn't until white people started buying rap, that
many in the Black middle class started to accept it.

Black people need to realize the type of influence the
European has had over their way of thinking.

Identity

The subject of skin color within the Black community
has been discussed in great detail over the years. It has
even been the subject of T.V. talk shows in the last few
years.

Still many don't understand the history of it. It goes
back to the time of slavery. It basically started because
the original light skin slaves were the product of white
masters sleeping with the Black female slaves. It's ironic,
many Blacks are admiring the light skin ones, and the
white masters were chasing the dark skin ones.

It is important to realize that the children of these relationships were often treated better by their white mas-
ter/parent. They weren't raised to be Field Slaves,
therefore they usually ended up working as House
Slaves or sometimes they were freed. They often learned

to read and write, and sometimes received training in a trade.

When they married, they were often paired up with other house slaves. If they were a female, sometimes another master would by her for use as a mistress.

Remember, the children of such unions were still considered slaves, and therefore Black. Economics was probably the main reason for this. Slaves were a very expensive and valuable commodity.

Whites in the south therefore considered a person Black if they had any drop of Black blood in them. They called this the one drop rule. Even if three of person's grandparents were white and one was Black, they were to be considered Black.

Anthropologists call this the hypo-descent rule. This means people of mixed race are denied the status of the dominant group. In other words, one drop of Black blood and a person would be considered Black, but to be white you had to be pure. African Americans still accept this rule without realizing how derogatory it truly is. African Americans are held to a different standard than all other races and ethnic groups. For example if a person is one fourth Native American he is not usually considered a Native American. Whites would accept him as white and he could assimilate. African Americans are the only ethnic group ever defined buy U.S. laws in such a way. More information on this subject can be found in the book by James F. Davis, *"Who Is Black: One Nations Defini-*

tion."

When slavery came to an end many of the light skin Blacks were already free, and as stated before, some were educated and had trades. This elevated status was often passed on from one generation to the next. It should be noted, that up until the 1960's the majority of the African American lawyers, ministers, and undertakers in the southern United States were light skin.

Although there was some toleration of white males sleeping with female slaves there was none for white females sleeping with male African American slaves.

At this time it is not clear if there is any relationship between this and the fact that many successful African American males have chosen white wives.

Family

What is clear is the affect all of this had on the African American family institution. African American men and women have been engaged in a power struggle that started with slavery and continues to this day.

With many masters willing to sleep with the female slaves, it afforded the African American female with more power than their male counterparts. Often, masters would develop feelings for their slave/mistress'. One of the most notable examples of this is the relationship between Thomas Jefferson and his slave Sally Hemmings.

The main reason we know of this case is because Jefferson is famous. He is the author of the American Declaration of Independence.

What is important to realize is this state of affairs continued after slavery. A perfect example would be the Strom Thurmond case.

Here we have a white politician, who publicly at one time vehemently opposed the civil rights movement in America. While privately had fathered a Black child, whom he continued to give financial support to.

There is no record of how many white Americans over the years secretly fathered Black children. Still, one can assume that some of the mothers of these children had some type of influence with the fathers. Influence no doubt that African American males could never hope to have.

Another source of social power for African American woman was the fact that many woman slaves were used as nannies. Therefore many whites were cared for in their early years by, and developed somewhat close emotional ties with African American women. Even though the male slaves sometimes enjoyed a close relationship with their masters and family, it didn't occur to the degree that it did for the women.

None of this is was good for the African American male's ego. How can it be, when it seems white society seems more trusting and respectful of African American woman than men.

African American woman have long been independent and self reliant. The more independent and self reliant they are, the bigger the strain on their relationship. It is no coincidence that many of the strongest most independent woman are just that, strong and independent.

This is a tough situation we find ourselves in. Women want equality, whereas men want to be treated like men. Whether a woman works or doesn't work, she still wants her mate to treat her like the woman of the house. On the other hand if a man doesn't work, how many women will treat him like the man of the house? This is not equal treatment. In fact it gives the woman some superiority.

Lasting relationships are built on many things; one of the most important is compromise. Sensing at some point there will be little or no compromising many people are reluctant to even make or keep a commitment. Some independence has to be given up for the sake of unity.

For example, the United States of America would be much weaker if it were the Independent States of America. The civil war is a good reminder of the results when unity is lacking.

Avoidance

There are certain people that should be avoided. Unity with theses individuals is more costly than it is worth. They are dream killers. They are the chronic pessimist. This individual can weaken your resolve. He or she will try to convince you that you can't accomplish a particular goal. Many dream killers have often had their dreams killed.

If you're observant you can often spot dream killers before they start working on you. They often see the world around them as a dark and negative place. In their opinion things are bad and are going to get worse. They will often tell you things like," unemployment and crime are on the rise; the economy is terrible; politicians are all corrupt; now's not the time to start a new business, buy a house or get a new car."

They have many complaints and very little that they are grateful for. They will often disagree with you for argument sake. This type of person will poison your mind if you spend too much time in their company. You should spend your time instead, with people who motivate you. Your associates should support your goals, and give you healthy, constructive criticisms.

The dream killer comes in many shapes and forms. Here are the three most common.

One type of dream killer is the person who is constantly unhappy. Remember, misery loves company. This person will try to drag you into their dark world. They probably won't be doing it intentionally; it's just that this mind set is contagious. Human beings need positive feed back. You would not continue doing something if the results were negative. Many of our actions are motivated by a prediction or hope of positive feed back. We pursue an education predicting it will yield a good paying job in the future. These predictions are often based on other people's results. If you are constantly exposed to an unhappy person, they may influence you to expect unpleasant results. In other words you will expect negative feed back. Bad expectations will not motivate you to attempt difficult tasks.

Another dream killer to be on guard for is the unlucky. Bad things just happen to him. He's the one who always gets caught when he does the wrong thing and fails when he does the right thing. Often times they're not bad people, they're just constantly in the wrong place at the wrong time. If you are with them, it's possible you are in the wrong place also.

Finally we come to the most dangerous person of all. The jealous/ envious one. For this dream killer it's personal. He actually wants something that you have; or wants to prevent you from getting what he has. In slang terms this person is known as a hater. This is the person who hopes you suffer a misfortune. They are happy when you are sad. They see your failure as their success. If there is a job opening, they won't tell you about it; but will go out of their way to talk negatively about you. Some times they kill more than just dreams. Jealousy and envy have been the cause of homicides since Cain killed Abel.

Education

One of the most deceptive links in the sociological chain, and therefore one of the most dangerous, is the American education system. Education is the acquiring of useful knowledge and skills. The basic ones are reading, writing, and arithmetic. U.S. schools also emphasize history and other social studies. A good education is vital.

Since the African first appeared on the American continent, he has been denied, equal access to education. The slaves were taught, just enough to serve master, but not enough to understand the world around them.

For example, they were taught English, but not how to read and write. They were taught the concept of Christianity, but not the concept of all men being created equal.

One hundred years later and the patterns are still continuing. Now Blacks are taught, go to school, get a good education and you will get a good job. They are told if you don't get a good education, you'll be working in a gas station, fruit and vegetable market, or some other low paying job.

African Americans work for others and make them rich. Meanwhile other immigrant groups take the jobs we don't want. They end up owning these businesses and passing them on to their children. African American are still taught to serve their masters, but not about the world around them.

This doesn't mean that a formal education is not important. It just highlights the difference between a formal education and a total education. To understand, lets go back to our description of education; the acquiring useful knowledge. Knowledge is useful if it benefit's the individual or society at large. An example of benefiting the individual is learning to count your change in the store. A doctor's education benefits society. These skills are usually learned in the formal setting of a school.

There are many beneficial skills not taught in schools, at least not in predominantly African American schools. Black children are not taught about writing checks and filling out deposit slips. Unless they major in business or accounting many grow into adults never having learned about the stock market. They don't know the difference between money markets and mutual funds. Meanwhile white children are learning these things. Sometimes in school, sometimes at home.

African Americans need to acquire this knowledge. The good thing is, it's not as hard as many think. One of the benefits of living in the United States is access to information. We have public and school libraries, bookstores, television, radio, and the Internet. A person can find information on any subject he chooses.

Always keep in mind though that they will try to keep the status quo and limit who has access to this knowledge. The reason, most successful revolutions and rebellions are led by the educated. Governments realize this all over the world. Saudi Arabia for instance has a free university to teach the Islamic religion to foreigners. The only requirement is that when you graduate you must leave the country. They recognize the danger of having a highly educated society.

The United States would rather bring in educated foreigners to meet their needs than educate the African Americans who are already here. They understand that most foreigners will have nothing but gratitude for America. On the other hand, if too many African Americans are educated at one time, the United States will have a serious problem on their hands.

Remember, knowledge is power. Acquire it, and you will acquire power.

If you don't do it for yourself, do it for your children. Don't expect a good education from a system that is designed and financed by others. This system is designed for their benefit not yours. They will teach your children how to stand in line, so they can give them fish. They won't teach them how to fish.

Deception

One of the ploys they use to keep this system going is deception.

This is done in many ways. The simplest is concealment. They simply don't tell us what they don't want us to know. They simply won't offer a particular course in the inner city schools, or the library won't have certain books. There's an old saying; 'if you want to hide something from a Black man, put it in a thick book.' The New York Times is a major U.S. newspaper. Their motto is all the news that's fit to print. It is a very large paper, with many pages. This newspaper contains a lot of valuable information. Many African Americans will look at it and be turned off by its shear size. What many don't realize is people don't usually read the entire New York Times. They tend to read the parts that have the information they require.

Another way they deceive African Americans is with distractions. Magicians do this in their acts all the time. They get you to look away from a certain thing, while they do something with it. This is also done to African Americans all the time.

Sports are a major distraction. This doesn't mean that sports aren't good. We all know the importance of exercise and being in good shape.

What we don't know is why the government will use tax dollars to build and support a major stadium. The same reason the Romans built the Coliseums. To distract the people. There are African Americans who can name the entire starting line up of their favorite team, but can't name three local elected officials. They can tell you how much their favorite player makes, but not how much money is in their child's school budget. They will argue why a certain player is over paid, and not discuss the fact that the teachers in their community are paid less than the ones in the suburbs.

It is important to realize, that human beings need to unwind sometimes. Sports, entertainment, and other leisure activities are vital to human mental and physical health. It is a problem though, when it is used to keep us from enquiring into certain subjects. This is the same thing parents do with their children. They buy them toys to play with, so that the parent can do his/her thing uninterrupted.

Another distraction is drugs. Heroin use exploded in the 60's. This coincided with the Black Power movement. Heroin in the 60's and 70's and crack cocaine in the 80's and 90's devastated the Black community. It was only after these drugs started reaching the suburbs that the so called war on drugs began.

The only way we can counter these deceptions is to expose them. This exposure is different than the one we use to attack institutional racism. When we expose institutional racism, we hope to make the racist stop their action. On the other hand deception dies with exposure. Once you know the truth it doesn't matter if the deceiver continues or not, he can no longer trick you.

White America has been deceiving Blacks for so long, the truth has been forgotten. For example; there's the myth that Blacks are lazy. They will define almost all other ethnic groups as hard working. If this statement were true, why were African Americans enslaved for nearly 250 years? Why didn't America get hard working Koreans, Chinese, or Mexicans to pick there cotton? Why would the white masters want lazy Black slaves? In fact, logic would say that the master was the lazy one, since the slave did all the work. In fact, Africans were the only group brought here specifically to work hard. Everyone else came for a better life.

Blacks need to point this out whenever they get a chance. We need to spread the truth, just like our enslavers spread the lies.

Priorities

Just knowing the truth is not enough. Knowledge without action is useless. There are certain things we need to do. How do we determine what needs to be done? How do we determine our priorities?

We begin by asking ourselves three questions.

(Note to reader, these questions are from the book: The 21 irrefutable Laws of Leadership)

1. What is required?

Food, shelter, and clothing. These are the basics. If we go deeper, we can add one more, security. Everyone needs to feel safe. If these basic needs are not met, life can be very miserable. Therefore the first priority is securing these necessities. First for ourselves, then for our families, and finally for our people.

2. What gives the greatest return?

These are the things that benefit us the most. This includes things like, getting a good education, working for a living, and treating people the way we want to be treated. Jesus is quoted in the New Testament as saying, 'do unto others as you would have them do unto you.' Eventually we are paid for whatever we do. The good for the good, the bad for the bad. So set priorities that benefit you and society.

3. What brings the greatest reward?

In other words, what makes you feel good in your heart. This includes things like being a good parent. Remember, it is important to realize, you can be a good parent even if your children don't live with you. How you treat your children when they are young helps to influence how they will treat you when you are old. Helping others also manifest good feelings in our heart. Being kind and courteous to others also helps us, remember, 'you reap what you sow.'

If we use these three questions as an outline, establishing our priorities becomes easier. This in turn makes it easier to pass them on to our children, which will increase their chances of becoming an honest and productive member of society. Otherwise the streets and greed set their priorities. Hanging out becomes more important than going to school. The opinions of their peers become more important than the opinions of parents, teachers, and potential employers. Making money becomes more important than how you make your money. If allowed to go unchecked, children tend to ignore the consequences of their actions.

Without proper priorities, a person has no main concerns. Therefore whatever happens is what happens. This is why so many so called middle class African American children are in prison. The parents did not set the child's priorities straight.

This affects the entire African community. This is one of the reasons many middle class Black neighborhoods, become so called ghettos in two to three generations.

Reparations

For many African Americans the new priority has become reparations for slavery. Reparations are payments for a wrong or injury.

It would be great if every African American was given a few million dollars for the labor of their ancestors. Of course this probably won't happen. How often does a thief voluntarily give back what he stole? On top of that, who would want to pay for his great grand father's treachery? Many white Americans become angry when they hear Blacks talk about reparations. They feel that slavery was so long ago Blacks should just forget about it. In the same breath they will tell people to remember the holocaust. It seems it's o.k. for whites to receive reparations, but Blacks should turn the other cheek. African Americans need to realize that white America does not feel obligated for slavery. If the whites who enslaved us didn't pay, why would their ancestors want to?

The American government has never even officially apologized for slavery much less admitted it was wrong.

According to Bruce Alpert in a Newhouse News Service story: Historians have long known that African-American slaves helped build both the Capitol and the White House, but Edward Hotaling, a historian and television reporter, recently uncovered proof that slaves constituted a majority of the 650 workers who built the structures, two of the most recognizable symbols of the nation's democratic heritage. Hotaling found pay stubs dating from the 1790s that show payments to slave owners but nothing to the laborers. One of the stubs, dated October 1795, calls for the payment of $5 a month to Joseph Farrah for "hire of his Negro, Charles."

Still they look at the Blacks who demand reparations

as beggars. It's important to realize, they lose respect for Blacks who ask them for anything. Remember the European built his empires on taking what he wanted from the non-whites of the world. Strength is what they respect.

The European Jews and Japanese Americans both received reparations for the way they were treated during World War Two. The only things African Americans have received are some Civil Rights laws and a couple of quotas. Which by the way, the current President, George Bush is trying to role back?

African Americans must realize that they can't make other races like them. They can force others to treat them with a certain degree of respect, but this won't change how they feel about Black people. Do you think other races care about how African Americans feel? There only concern is how Blacks spend there money, where we live, and that young Black men stay away from their daughters. African Americans should stop debating with white America over the issue of reparations. America knows Blacks want them and America knows that the slaves were never compensated. What America won't do is let Blacks win the argument over reparations. White Americans will never willingly part with that much money. To make this happen African Americans need to increase America's vulnerability.

Keys to power

A very important aspect of power is winning through action, not through argument. Arguing often leads to what is called a Pyrrhic victory.

Pyrrhus was a king in ancient Greece. He is most famous for the way he won a particular battle. Even though he had won the battle, he lost most of his men in combat. No one can afford too many wins like that.

Winning through argumentation often leads to this type of victory. There are often resentments and ill will left over after an argument or fight. If we have to convince the United States to give us anything, it means they didn't want to do it.

Instead, we should win through our actions. We should put our selves in a position where that would make them want to pay us.

Martin Luther King and others did just that. Not by marching, and demonstrating, and being thrown in jail. They did it by embarrassing America. Here was the United States trying to fight for freedom and democracy in Vietnam, and their own citizens did not have it at home. The world was watching, and the U.S. was vulnerable to international opinion.

Boycotts also expose vulnerability. If you don't treat people right, they can spend their money elsewhere. This has proven to be a very effective tool.

African Americans need to be more strategic. Instead

of asking for things like reparations, they should be planning a strategy to **get** them. They are asking for reparations, and in the mean time, the percentage of Blacks living in poverty has risen from 26% in 1969 to 30% in 1986 alone. Even though the Black upper-class has increased, Black people in general, are worse off now than they were when the Civil Rights movement was in full swing.

The Europeans have a strategy to keep us in our place. It is to keep us divided. They have fought against each other in many wars, but they are united in their dealings with people of African decent. Now that Black people realize their strategy, it's time develop a counter strategy. A strategy that has at its core Black unity. Remember unity starts with strong family values. It is important, because if families can't stay united, a whole race doesn't stand a chance.

Chapter 4
Psychological

Webster defines psychology as the science of mind and behavior.

Self-esteem

In order to keep African Americans enslaved as long as they did, the Europeans had to lower the collective Black self-esteem. At some point the slaves would have to learn to accept their position. The only alternatives were, escape, insanity, or death.

Many Africans chose these options rather than submitting to slavery. The majority though, lived their lives in servitude.

There are many theories about how this was done. To better understand this issue, let us examine some of the facts.

First generation slaves were usually kidnapped and separated from people and loved ones. No one can doubt that this in itself was a traumatic ordeal. Then there was the "boat" ride to America.

Also known as the Middle Passage. The death rates on many ships often approached 50 percent. The slaves were packed in cargo holds sometimes two or more layers deep. The conditions were unsanitary as well as inhumane. They lay or crouched in their own excrement and blood. They were forced to endure these smells as well as the odor of their fellow Africans who sometimes had died but were still left chained in the cargo hold. This usually lasted any where from a few weeks to a couple of months. No one can doubt that this was a traumatic ordeal.

After the Middle Passage, most Africans ended up in Brazil or the Caribbean, where they were sold in auctions. This is when the seasoning process took place. This was to make sure they could survive the different diseases that existed in the Americas.

To top it off, they were issued orders, in a language they didn't understand and the whip was the exclamation point at the end of every sentence. By the time the slaves reached the Carolinas they were suffering from Post Traumatic Syndrome.

Nowadays if you put a person thru half of this they'd be able to sue for millions of dollars.

Imagine what these first generation slaves taught their children. How much self esteem could they pass on? How can one truly posses self-esteem, when another man is his master. Imagine being stripped of all that you own, including your name and language. What kind of pride can you instill in your children? What kind of emotional security can you instill in them when master can separate the family at a whim?

Africans endured this for over two hundred years. Then came the first hundred years of "freedom." During this time Blacks were taught in school that Africa was a big jungle filled with cannibals. They were led o believe that Egypt and the Pyramids weren't even a part of African history. Even though the truth has being taught for the last sixty or so years, many Blacks will not accept it.

The author remembers discussing with an African coworker the theory that African mariners were here before the Europeans, the coworker refused to believe it. He asked the author, "Where did you hear this silliness?" When he was told to look into the book, "They Came Before Columbus," by Ivan Van Sertima, he frowned and just walked away.

This brings us back to our analogy of virtual chains. This African brother's mind was in shackles. He had a good paying job, and it seemed he didn't want to jeopardize it with dangerous talk. Lest the white boss became angry.

So this brings us to the question, is it better to be a well off slave, or a poor free man?

If you asked a poor white southerner this in 1835, he'd have probably said freedom is better. Whereas if you had asked a house slave, he'd probably go tell master, or at the very least he'd probably say something like, "hush that fool talk."

Propaganda

How did the enslavers get us to think like this, and more importantly, how do they continue to do it?

The answer is two fold, with brainwashing and propaganda. Even though they are similar, there are slight differences. They are as follows;

Propaganda is the spreading of information -facts, rumors, half-truths, and lies- to influence the way people think and behave. The person using propaganda most often hides their true intentions. Propaganda differs from education. Education tries to show many sides of an issue, those for and against. Whereas propagandist wants you believe their way.

Brainwashing on the other hand, the person lets you know how they want you to think and behave. To accomplish this they use torture, forced starvation, and separation from friends and loved ones. Does this sound familiar?

As stated earlier, the first generation of slaves were suffering from Post Traumatic Syndrome. It's easy to manipulate the mind of people in this condition. This trauma used with the right techniques, had a brainwashing effect on the newly captured Africans. Ad to this the fact that America was far from Africa. Therefore, even if they escaped, they probably would not make it back to Africa. This system was used to keep newly enslaved Africans in line. For those born into slavery and later generations they needed a different system, they needed propaganda.

The tools of propaganda:

1. The agent.
Basically everything the master told his slave had one purpose, to make him a better slave. Sometimes the master would deliver the propaganda himself. For propaganda to be most effective though, they needed, an agent, someone the slaves would trust. This was often their parents. The parent who came from Africa was a good tool for the master. If he was enslaved long enough to raise children, he probably had given up hope of trying to escape. In a way then, this meant he had accepted his condition. Also it usually meant that at some level he accepted the European as a superior. He would be used to pass this way of thinking down to his children. To some degree this continues to this day. This will be discussed in greater detail later.

The House slave was also used as an agent by the enslavers. He knew that if he behaved right, he would keep his privileges. This included telling the other slaves how to act. He would say things like, there is no use in trying to escape. He also doubled as a spy, he would bring back information to the master. The majority of the major planned slave revolts were exposed by house slaves.

Another type of agent which is very controversial is

the religious leader. Antebellum Black preachers spoke about turning the other cheek and waiting for a pie in the sky. In other words, be content and your reward will be given in Heaven. The issue is not if Christianity is true, the issue is how this served the enslavers. This is why they often chose the Black preachers. Often he'd be a House Slave or at least someone with a House Slave mentality. It's important to realize that the agent often didn't know he is being used to influence the people.

If the propaganda became exposed or disbelieved, the slaves would often become angry with the agent. Whether it be the House Slave for being masters front man, or their parents for accepting their condition. The agent becomes the scapegoat, while the master develops a new strategy.

In his book "The Prince," Machiavelli said, "The prince (master) may openly and conspicuously bestow awards and honors and public offices; but he should have his agents carry out all actions that make a man un-popular, such as punishments, denunciations, dismissals, and assassinations.

This is why masters often had overseers or other slaves giving orders or doing the actual whipping of dis-obedient slaves.

The whipping and executing of slaves was also a type of propaganda, sociologist call it propaganda of the deed. The main propose was not to punish the slave, but to keep other slaves from doing what he/she did.

2. Symbols

Propagandist use signs and symbols to deliver their message. The signs can be words, pictures, or actions; basically a sign is anything that has a meaning to someone. Symbols are signs that have special meanings to particular people.

The enslavers mixed certain symbols with four other variables to get and keep a slave mentality effect.

The first would be predisposition, this was what the slaves already thought about themselves and their predicament. They would tell the young slaves that they didn't deserve to be free, these children would then see their parents accepting slavery. In modern times it works the same. Black children will hear, "Blacks don't want to work, they'd rather be on welfare." This child may look to his family and neighbors and see two or three generations on welfare, and think that he has no choice but to receive it also. This is not to say that whites are not on welfare, it just points out that they hear a different message.

The second variable used is economics. Black children may hear something like; "The only way African Americans can get out of the ghetto is to sell drugs." This child will then look around the neighborhood and see drug dealers with nice cars, clothes , and jewelry.

The third is physical. This takes many forms. Africans were whipped if they didn't behave correctly. After physical slavery this changed to Lynching. It's important to note that the first set of race riots in this country, consisted of white mobs attacking Blacks. A Black man may have heard, "you don't deserve the right to vote." If you add this to his fear of being lynched he might not push for his voting rights.

The fourth is social pressure from whites as well as Blacks. This would be white people denying jobs or housing to someone because he is Black. It could also be other Blacks saying things like, don't make trouble for us, stay out of white people's business, you know they ain't gonna let no Blacks live on that side of town etc.

As you can see propaganda is still used today. It is much more sophisticated and the effects are probably even greater than during physical slavery.

Separate but Equal

Black people have to realize that this propaganda wasn't just for African Americans. These techniques were also used to convince white people that Blacks were an inferior race. They needed this to satisfy their conscience, and justify their treatment of the Africans.

This propaganda even affected the whites who were against slavery. They wanted African Americans to be free and equal citizens, as long as the majority of them stayed in the south. The attitudes of northern whites changed after large numbers of Blacks started to emigrate from the south.

In time Black ghettos started springing up all over the country. African Americans had there own churches, schools, hospitals, etc.

In the south this was accomplished by Jim Crow laws. In the north they used unwritten laws which are still followed today. Blacks move in, whites move out.

Black culture is held to a lower standard than that of white America. This can be easily seen in music and music videos.

You will often see African American woman referred to in these videos as bitches and hoes. You will see African American men bragging about selling drugs or calling them selves pimps. Many videos top it off with drug use.

How long do you think these videos would be shown if it were young white girls being called bitches and hoes by a weed smoking pimp?

Why do Blacks tolerate many things that white America won't? The reason is they have been programmed to interpret things differently.

Perception

There are many theories of psychology. This section of the book will be based on the theory of cognitive behavior therapy. The basic idea behind this theory is that people base their feelings on how they have been taught to interpret reality.

Many African Americans have a distorted view of reality. They are using lies and myths to draw seemingly logical conclusions about the world in which they live. Often these false conclusions will bring about inappropriate behavior.

These false conclusions are actually limited thinking patterns. They are attempted judgments, which are made without examining all of the evidence. They are Cognitive Distortions.

Not only do these distortions affect African Americans as a group, on a social level, they contribute to low self esteem on a personal level.

Propaganda planted the seeds for these thought patterns. One of the main techniques of propaganda is repetition. I f a person hears something enough times they will start to believe it in spite of contrary evidence.

There are eight major Cognitive Distortions. The first eight are based on the lies that Blacks have been taught about themselves as a group and as individuals. The last one is an outgrowth of the others and often is the cause of the violence that plagues the Black community.

Cognitive Distortions

1. Overgeneralization.
When you over generalize, you make broad, general

conclusions based on a single incident or piece of evidence. For example, suppose you go on a job interview and don't get the job. From this you may conclude, "no one will hire me."

This type of thinking constricts your universe. Actually it is the opposite of the scientific method. Instead of examining all of the evidence to draw a conclusion, people will take one or two facts and make that the rule. People will hear about a Wall Street broker ripping off a client, and then assume that the entire stock market is a rip off.

Here's an example of overgeneralization on a social level: It's a fact that Black neighborhoods have a disproportionately high level of violent crime. The one who over generalizes may conclude that Black people are more violent than white people.

Let's examine this more closely. We can start by considering more facts.

There are people in Iraq and Afghanistan, who have seen first hand the devastation of American bomber planes. For the most part these planes are piloted by middle class whites. The people in these countries and many like them see American whites as the most dangerous and violent people on earth. Many consider Europeans in general a warlike people.

In fact, in the last one hundred years, every major war except one has involved Europeans. In World War Two alone forty to fifty million people died.

Some may say, look at the tribal and civil wars in Africa. Even these take on a different appearance when we examine more of the facts. The borders and nations of all African countries except Ethiopia were defined by Europeans. At one time all these nations were colonies of the Europeans. It appears that when they drew these borders, they put tribes and religious groups together that did not belong together. It seems not only do Europeans like war, but they like watching a good one too.

The killing of six million Jews by Nazi Germany and its allies is another example of the violent nature of some Europeans. Then there's the treatment of Native Americans and the Aborigines of Australia.

Do people of African decent still seem more violent than Europeans?

Another generalization is based on the high unemployment rate for African American males. Many people will conclude that Black males are lazy. When we look at more of the facts, we see a different picture. Even if we don't consider the discriminatory reasons for higher Black unemployment, there is still overwhelming evidence to put this lie to rest. SLAVERY. As was stated earlier Africans were not enslaved for their laziness.

Black people will often generalize that all white people stick together. They base this on the apparent fact that whites are generally united in certain attitudes about Blacks. This is where their unity ends. The two most devastating wars this world has ever seen were basically fought in Europe, amongst Europeans.

We can see that overgeneralization on a social level constricts ones view of the world. It limits ones ability to draw logical conclusions about the world in which one lives. African Americans who don't read and keep up with, community and current events are often forced to "imagine" what's going on in the world around them.

This limited thought pattern is also crippling on a personal level also. It can limit a person's self-esteem. If a child fails one class in school, he may believe that he is not as capable as other children. This type of thinking often forces people to not to make any attempts after one failure. They don't realize that all human beings have short comings. They've never been told the only true failure is the one who has stopped trying.

Parents have a strong influence on their children's self-esteem. This in turn shapes the child's view, of how he sees the world and his place in it. For example, if you are constantly yelling at and threatening your children, they will have a tendency to view the world as a hostile place.

Black people must learn to recognize when they are using this type of thinking. One clue that you may be over generalizing is the use of certain generalized words. These are words like; all, every, none, never, always, everybody, and nobody. This doesn't mean that every time you use one of these words you are over generalizing.

There are times when these words are appropriate.

For example, "all human beings, will eventually die," "every one of my coworkers lives within 250 miles of the job." These generalizations may be based on number of verifiable facts. It's when you base your conclusion on one or two pieces of evidence, that you open your self up to overgeneralization.

This would be sayings like; "all Blacks are lazy," "all Jews are cheap," "all white people stick together," etc.

Another aspect of generalization is global labeling. This is when you take one characteristic of a person, place, or thing, and apply that characteristic to the entire thing. For instance, Republicans are racist.

Even though there may be some Republicans who are racist, to apply this trait to all of them is over generalizing. It ignores the fact that there is probably some evidence to the contrary.

2. Filtering.

This type of thinking is similar to tunnel vision. You only see or notice one side of the story. It is usually the negative side. For example: A woman goes to a party. She is wearing a new dress that really makes her look good. A few of her girlfriends even give her some compliments on it. She's wearing nice high heel shoes and gets some compliments on them also. On top of that, she has just had her hair done. She is approached by many women, who ask her where did she get it done, so they can go there too. She feels like the belle of the ball. Then while dancing she stumbles. Her boyfriend says, 'it's because her heels are too high and inappropriate for this type of party." she suddenly feels that she looks like a fool. She has filtered out all the good comments she has heard during the night. She can only remember what her boyfriend said.

Filtering is closely related to overgeneralization. The difference is slight. With overgeneralization you draw a conclusion from one fact. Whereas with filtering you know many facts, you just choose to ignore the ones that don't support what you believe.

Filtering can lead to self-fulfilling prophesy. If you only see and remember the bad, your actions will reflect that. In time you will subconsciously work towards what you think will happen. Many of us have had a coworker who thinks the boss or another coworker is out to get him. All he sees is what they do to harm him. He starts to do things that always end up landing him in trouble. Eventually the boss has to let him go, but this person never sees the part he has played in the whole affair.

A perfect example of filtering on a social level is the American education systems view on history. Fortunately, much of the filtering has been exposed. Many people realize that there is much hypocrisy and inaccuracy in the way history is taught in America. We are taught that Christopher Columbus discovered America. What's filtered out is it's not a discovery if someone is already living there.

American history teaches that the Native Americans gave up this land through various treaties. What is not taught is that the Native Americans, like the Africans did not have the same concept of borders that the Europeans did. They believed if different people were not at war, they could share the land. Therefore as long as there was enough for everybody, friendly tribes shared the same area. The European had no such concept.

Propaganda is a type of filtering. It is a way to get people to see things a certain way and to ignore others. For example, television and the movies were used to convince people that Africa was wilderness filled with savages. When many think of Africa they think of Tarzan. An image comes up of a white man yodeling and a bunch of Africans hiding from him in fear. This image is so engrained in our minds that most people find it hard to believe that empires existed in Africa.

This filtering of history is part of the reason Europeans can't understand how the Pyramids of Egypt were built. They can't accept the fact that Africans (yes the Egyptians were African, and not European), had built these structures when Europeans hadn't even started building homes yet. Therefore there must be some other explanation. Many would rather think that aliens from another planet and not the Africans are responsible for the Pyramids.

Exactly who the Egyptians were/are has been confused through this filtering of history. To answer this question we can look to Lerone Bennett Jr., from his monumental book "Before The Mayflower." He tells us that the Egyptians identified themselves in hieroglyphics with three colors, Black, reddish-brown, and yellow. They used the color white to portray foreigners.

Social filtering, like generalization constricts ones view of the world. It is type of ignorance. A person is either taught or forced to ignore certain aspects of the world around them. When this happens there thoughts and actions are based on only one side of an issue. If these are based on incorrect information, it often leads to inappropriate behavior.

Human beings are limited as to how much information they can process. For this reason we are forced to filter out some of the information we receive. This can become a problem when we filter out whole categories of information. When this is done on a personal level filtering can lead to low self-esteem or denial.

Many people with low self-esteem use their minds like a voice activated tape recorder. It is activated by certain types of stimuli. These bits of information reinforce the core ideas behind the person's low self opinion. Their minds become aroused by examples of rejection, unfairness, loss, etc. They tune out the good things. For these people the glass is always half empty rather than half full.

People who suffer from denial on the other hand, filter out certain information to protect their ego or self-esteem. This type of filtering is used when people can't handle the truth. It can be a woman who has evidence that her husband is cheating, but she refuses to acknowledge the fact. Then you have the parents whose child is using drugs. Everyone notices it, but the parents are blind to the fact.

Think back about a recent social gathering or conversation. If all you can remember are unpleasant events, the chances are you are filtering out some of the good. To escape this type of thinking, people must remind themselves that almost nothing is all good or all bad.

The author met a young woman who was laid off from her job. She had received the news on a Friday afternoon. She said, "The weekend that followed was the worst of my life." She was depressed and felt like a failure. Monday morning with no job to go to, her depression worsened. She felt as if there wasn't any hope and she couldn't go on with life. Tuesday morning she was the happiest woman alive. She had been fired from a job in the World Trade Center four days prior to the 9/11 attack. We must try to tell ourselves, every cloud has a silver lining.

3. Polarized Thinking.

This is when you think of things in terms of either right of wrong. There is no middle ground. Polarized thinking is similar to filtering. The difference is, instead of seeing one side you see two. The problem with this kind of thinking is there are often more than two sides to an issue. Polarized thinking leaves little room for compromise.

This limited thought pattern is being applied to a major issue today, reparations. It has become either reparations are paid or they aren't. For both sides of the issue it has become a win or lose proposition, with neither side wanting to be the loser.

If African Americans considered more options, the American government may be willing to reach a compromise. First of all African Americans can start by realizing that there are more than just money involved in the whole subject of reparations.

The American government would first have to officially recognize and admit that slavery was wrong. How can African Americans expect reparations, if the U.S. government doesn't even recognize the wrong that was committed? America has to be slowly coaxed into redressing the wrongs to Black America. You have to crawl before you can walk.

Polarization on a personal level greatly influences self-esteem. Everything becomes either/or. Someone may see themselves as good or bad, intelligent or stupid, fit or overweight. People who are trapped into this type of thinking usually end up looking at themselves negatively.

4. Control Fallacies.

Control fallacies put people in control of the universe. There are two variations to this type of thinking. In the first one people feel they have control over everything that happens to them. In the second type they think everyone but them is control.

African Americans tend to fall into one category or the other. There are some who blame all their problems on Europeans, and others who blame themselves.

There are many African Americans who blame there unemployment on "the white man." The fact that this individual chose to drop out of school or isn't actively looking for a job doesn't cross their mind. It often becomes easier to blame others than to accept responsibility for our action.

Then you have the Black people who blame African Americans themselves for their problems. It seems these people don't take into account that all the constitutional amendments and civil rights laws were written for a reason. It as if they feel racism and discrimination never existed. Every situation is different. Some things you control, some are controlled by other, and everything else is under the authority of a higher power. Knowing the difference helps us to place credit or blame where it's due.

It is important that African Americans realize how detrimental control fallacies can be to their self-esteem.

The person who thinks they're in control blames themselves for everything that goes wrong in their life. If they ask a friend for a lift somewhere and the friend loses their wallet; they blame themselves. If a spouse cheats on them, they blame themselves. They tell themselves if I'd had been a better husband and not worked so many hours. It never occurs to them that their spouse cheated because she made a choice to cheat. Others may blame you for their choices, but if you haven't held a gun to their head it's their choice. Often the person with control fallacies thinks they're a jinx.

Worse off is the person who thinks everyone beside them is in control. The very nature of this type of thinking leaves one feeling hopeless and helpless. This person feels they are at the whim of whomever. This person feels they have no control of their life. Someone is always making them do something or feel bad. People stuck in this type of thought pattern need to realize that they have power and are the most influential people in their own lives.

Many twelve step organizations teach their members they are powerless over drugs and alcohol.[6] Care must be taken not to misunderstand how powerlessness is used in this context. What is actually meant is an addict is powerless over drugs if they attempt to use them. This powerlessness extends to anything that brings them closer to drugs or alcohol. On the other hand, if they stay away from drugs using the twelve steps they become

---

[6] There are also twelve step groups devoted to gambling, sex, and many other things that people abuse.

empowered. This definition must be understood. Otherwise people will use powerlessness as an excuse for inaction.

5. Personalization.

Personalization comes in two forms. The first type is to think everything is connected to you. It is similar to paranoia. This is more than just thinking about you first. It is putting you at the center of the universe. Everything that happens is some how connected to you. It seems that, if you analyze all events correctly, they will relate to you.

Many African Americans take everything white America does personally. This often brings about inappropriate behavior. For example, a business decides not to locate in an urban area because they can't afford the rent. Blacks who are affected by this may cry racism. They organize protest and level accusations at the business. All of this is inappropriate, because the move is economic and has nothing to do with racism.

African Americans need to learn the difference between cause and effect. Just because something affects you does not mean it was done because of you. The cause of a business move is a desire for profits. The effect may be loss of jobs in the minority community.

It is human nature to judge people by their actions and not by their intentions. In fact the more the action affects someone, the less they are concerned with intentions.

This is where analytical thinking should come into play. The U.S. justice system is supposed to use both actions and intentions in rendering a verdict. For example a person's intention can mean the difference between 1st degree murder, manslaughter, or an accident. Thus the intentions determine what crime if any has been committed. On the other hand if someone's actions cause enough damage, they can be accused of negligence. In that case it does not matter what their intentions were.

Personalization sometimes makes people feel something is done because of them and it doesn't even have anything to do with them. A man's wife may complain about rising prices because of inflation. The husband may think that she is implying that he doesn't make enough money. Then there is the mother who blames herself when her children misbehave.

The second type consists of comparing your self to other people. It consists of Statements or thoughts like, "I'm not as good looking as him," or "He's smarter than me." Sometimes these thoughts are in your favor, "I'm stronger than him," "My jobs better than his," etc.

Continuously comparing yourself with others shows problems with self worth. If you constantly do this, sooner of later someone will be judged better off than you. This is turn will even lower your self-esteem.

6. Mind reading.

This is when you assume to know what a person thinks or feels.

Many people will fool themselves into thinking they are using logic to draw their conclusions as to what others are thinking. There is a least one way to test if this assumption is based on logic or mind reading. It may be based on logic if you have a number of possibilities as to what someone is thinking. It is the cognitive distortion of mind reading if you think know what the person is thinking.

Almost everyone has wrongly guessed what another person was thinking. How many times have you thought a girl liked you, but found out otherwise when you asked her out.

It becomes a problem when you often base decisions on your assumptions. This is especially true if you suffer from low self-esteem or depression. When you mind read you tend to think that people think like you. Therefore if you think poorly of yourself, you will think that others feel the same way. This often causes you to act in inappropriate ways.

You can tell if you are mind reading by asking your self one simple question, "How do I know what another person is thinking? If your answer is, "I can just tell," "I have a hunch," "I've got a feeling," it's safe to assume you are mind reading.

Remember feelings aren't facts and hunches aren't evidence. We can never really know what a person is thinking or feeling. Even when they tell us their thoughts they could be lying. If we could mind read we'd never be cheated and would always know which girl to ask out on a date.

7. Should/judgments.

This is when you think people should behave and do things a certain way. When people don't do things your way you judge them negatively. These judgments also extend to appearances and opinions. When people don't do things the way you feel they should you become irritated.

The media and the education system have been used to program Black People into certain types of behavior. When people don't behave in these pre programmed ways they are judged to be peculiar. This is why drug dealers and thugs are idolized; and good students are often looked at as strange.

This type of thinking is also learned in childhood. It often comes from being raised by judgmental parents. These types of parents are constantly judging other people, as well as telling the child that he/she must behave and think in a particular way.

The problem with judging is, at some point we begin to judge ourselves. It's like playing Russian roulette. The first couple of judgments may not harm you; in fact they may make you feel good about yourself. Then all of a sudden you judge someone to be better off than you.

This is when the shoulds start to chip away at your self-esteem.

Remember, in the Bible it says, "Judge not or so you shall be judge."

When people judge themselves they should ask, "Are these rules realistic." Sometimes we expect more from others and ourselves than is possible. When we think in terms of shoulds, we are actually thinking that we shouldn't make mistakes. It's as if we forget the fact that human beings are not perfect.

8. Emotional Reasoning.

This is probably the most dangerous of all the cognitive distortions. In this limited thinking pattern you actually don't think at all. In this chaotic world your feelings become your reality. You base actions on how you feel, instead of a logical interpretation of reality.

For instance, a Black man is parking his new car at the mall, when another car, pulling out bangs into him. How many times have you seen Blacks jump out of their cars yelling and cursing? Sometimes even coming to blows over minor fender benders. The fact that the insurance company is probably going to fix his car doesn't influence him at all. Instead his behavior is determined by his emotions.

Emotional reasoning is the reason that accidentally stepping on someone's foot at a party can turn into gunfire. The person feels "dissed," therefore he is "dissed."

The fact that it may have been an accident doesn't matter. In a world of emotional reasoning, feelings become more important than facts.

The effects of this type of thinking on personal self-esteem can be devastating. You may feel like you can't get a job or you may feel like selling drugs is the only way you can earn a living. These feelings become your reality and prevent you from trying.

To combat this we must learn to not act on our feelings. Instead we have to figure out what is causing these feelings and counter act it. We must resist acting on any feeling that doesn't lead to life enhancing behavior.

New Habits

The key to breaking this psychological chain is to establish new habits. Habits are those things you do regularly without thinking. This includes things like the way you brush your teeth, to how you react when someone stares at you on the subway.

Your habits will determine your future. Individually and as a people, Blacks need to develop new habits.

As stated earlier, we need to become more producer orientated and less consumer orientated. It is also important that African Americans become thriftier and save more of their income. Just doing these alone will greatly enhance your quality of your economic life.

To enhance the sociological and psychological aspects of the Black community one thing must be remembered, no judgments. They must be stopped. All of the distorted ways of thinking that were mentioned have some aspect of judgmental behavior in them. Also being judgmental makes it harder for Blacks to unite as a people.

Instilling these habits into your children should also be a priority. Think of it as an investment in your family's future. Remember to be successful you must develop successful habits.

We must take the bad habits that have been programmed into us and turn them around. It usually takes about a month a daily practice to develop a new habit. Dropping the bad habits will be a little harder, but the key is not to give up.

Remember failure is not an option. If you stumble and fall back into bed in the morning do you go back to sleep? No, you regain your balance and get up. This is the attitude we should develop in all our affairs.

Change may seem unnecessary, scary, corny or just plain impossible. What Blacks must realize is that without change, progress is impossible.

Conclusion

There is one more thing that can help Blacks achieve power in the United States, volunteer work. If Blacks took an each one, teach one attitude, we could accomplish miracles. Successful middle and upper class African Americans need to volunteer their time to community based organizations. Yes it's hard, the people who are helped often seem ungrateful, and no one has the spare time, but the sacrifice is needed. In order to get a little further one must sacrifice and go a little further.

The Jews have done it with organizations like B'nai B'rith, and there are many Black orientated organizations that desperately need the help. The problem with many of the "Black American" organizations is they have become just jobs for the people who work in them. When this happens, people do just enough to get paid and little more. Many of these organizations have become bureaucracies that the average African American is unfamiliar with. The sad part is that many who are familiar with these organizations often feel alienated from them. If these organizations were helped by successful volunteers, they could gain a new vibrancy.

GLOSSARY

Amendment: A change to a legal document especially the U.S. Constitution.

Antebellum: Before the U.S. Civil War.

Anthropology: The study of the human race, especially human culture and human development.

Apartheid: The racist political system of South Africa from 1948 to the early 1990's. It gave different ethnic groups different rights, with Europeans getting special privileges.

Blacks: People of African decent.

Census: An official count of the population, usually done by the government.

Capital Goods: Goods used to produce other goods rather than being sold to consumers.

Congress: The governing and lawmaking body of the U.S. government. It consists of the House of Representatives and the Senate.

Congressman- woman: A member of the House of Representatives.

Constitution: A usually written statement outlining the basic laws of country or state.

Economics: The study of the production, distribution and consumption of goods and services.

Electoral College: The group, *elected* by the voters to choose the President and Vice President.

Emancipation Proclamation: The proclamation issued by Abraham Lincoln that declared freedom for all slaves in states in rebellion against the federal government.

Federal Reserve Bank: One of 12 reserve banks that regulates banks, helps determine interest rates, and oversees the money supply.

Government: A group of people who have the power to make and enforce the laws of a country or area.

Grandfather Clause: A law that allowed illiterate whites to vote because their grandfathers voted. While at the same time demanded that Blacks could only vote if they could read and write.

History: What has happened in the past, or a study of what has happened in the past.

House of Representatives: Lower house of the U.S. Congress. It's members are elected to 2 year terms.

Indentured Servant: An immigrant to the U.S. who agreed to work for a number of years in return for room board and transportation cost to America.

Jim Crow: The Southern practice of discriminating against Black people, especially in public institutions, e.g. schools, hospitals, etc.

Judge- Supreme Court: A judge is an official who determines the law in a court case. The Supreme Court is the highest court in the U.S. It has the last say in interpreting the law.

Law: The rules and regulation of a country or society, that have a system of enforcement.

Literary Test: A reading and writing test that was given to Blacks who tried to vote in the Southern United States. At that time most Blacks could not read well and therefore failed the test and weren't allowed to vote.

Market Price: The price that the majority of people are paying for something.

Media: The different means of mass communication. It includes television, newspapers, radio, and the internet.

Political Science: The study of political organizations, especially governments.

Poll Tax: A tax that must be paid in order to vote.

Psychology: The science that deals with the human mind and human behavior.

President: The chief political officer or a republic, for ex ample the President of the United States of America.

Reparations: Compensation for a wrong. Also something that is done to bring about amends.

Senator: A member of a senate, for example a member of the U.S. Senate.

Self-Esteem: Confidence in your own worth as an Individual.

Sharecropper: A tenant farmer who farms the land and shares what he produces with the land owner. Also a farmer who borrows money and pays it back with what he grows on his farm.

Social Science: The study of society and how people

relate individually and as a group. It includes many fields, for example Anthropology, Economics, Political Science, and Sociology to name a few.

Sociology: A branch of social science that deals with the behavior of individuals and groups in a society.

Stock Exchange: An organized market where brokers meet to buy and sell shares of stocks.

INDEX

119

References

Anderson, C., Ed.D. (1994). *Black Labor White Wealth*. PowerNomics Corporation of America.

Bennett, L., Jr. (1993). *Before the Mayflower A history of Black America* (6th Revised Ed.). New York: Penguin Books. (Original work published 1962)

Boldt, L. G. (2001). *How to be, do, or have anything*. Ten Speed Press.

Canfield, J., Hansen, M. V., & Hewitt, L. (2000). *The power of focus*. Deerfield Beach, FL: Health Comunications.

Chideya, F. (1995). *Don't believe the hype Fighting cultural misinformation about African Americans*. New York: Plume.

Covey, S. R. (1989). *The 7 habits of highly effective people*. New York: Fireside Simon & Schuster.

Davis, F. J. (1991). *Who is Black? One nation's definition*. University Park, Pennsylvania: The Pennsylvania State University Press.

Dixit, A. K., & Nalebuff, B. J. (1991). *Thinking Strategically*. New York: W.W. Norton & Company.

Greene, R. (1998). *The 48 laws of power*. New York: Penguin Books.

Haskins, J., & Butts, H. F., M.D. (1973). *Psychology of Black language*. New York: Hippocrene Books.

Maxwell, J. C. (1998). *The 21 irrefutable laws of leadership*. Nashville: Thomas Nelson Publishers.

McKay, M., Ph.D., & Fanning, P. (1992). *Self-esteem*. Oakland, CA: New Harbinger Publications.

Minchinton, J. (1993). *Maximum self-esteem The hand book for reclaiming your sense of self-worth*. Arnford House, Publishers.

Reader, J. (1999). *A biography of the continent Africa*. New York: Vintage Books. (Original work published 1997)

Robbins, A. (1986). *Unlimited power*. New York: Free Press.

Stanley, T. J., Ph.D. (2001). *The millionaire mind*. KansasCity: Andrews McMeel Publishing.